THE ART OF PROMPT ENGINEERING

For the Solo Founder

A Practical Guide to Designing, Building, and Launching Your First Web App with AI Coding

by

Tarek Kamal

June 2026

First Edition
Published by Tarek Kamal
ISBN: 979-8-234-13194-2

This book is based on the author's personal hands-on experience designing, building, testing, securing, and launching a software-as-a-service platform using AI-assisted coding tools over a period of approximately a year. The explanations, methods, frameworks, documentation approaches, examples, workflows, and lessons described in this book reflect the author's own experience, judgment, selection, organization, and expression.

The author has developed and presents original approaches for using prompt engineering in large, long-running AI-assisted software projects, including techniques intended to reduce hallucination, preserve project continuity, recover from deteriorating or "dying" AI chat sessions, and improve the reliability of AI-assisted design, coding, testing, documentation, deployment, quality assurance, and security work. The author also introduces and explains the concept of "LLM Psyche" as a practical mental model for understanding how large language models behave in extended project conversations and how that understanding can be used to write better prompts.The author also introduces 'Isolated Context Methodology' of having 'virtual engineering teams' to break up a large AI chat conversation into smaller topic focused conversations to reduce hallucination and improve quality of responses from the LLMs.

Artificial intelligence tools, including ChatGPT, Gemini, You.com, and other AI platforms, were used as assistive tools for editing, formatting, research support, review, and refinement of the manuscript. The author retained control over the book's concepts, structure, explanations, examples, conclusions, and final editorial decisions.

For permissions or inquiries, contact:

tarek7@live.com

To my mother and father.

Table of Contents

Introduction

The cost barrier for building software has collapsed, thanks to AI, but the barrier to production-grade quality can still be high. For product managers, system architects, and tech-savvy innovators, generative AI is a gift for taking a business idea from zero to one. Yet, most Solo Founders fail because their ideas lack true business value or they lack a good understanding of Prompt Engineering and Software Engineering concepts. This frequently leads to fragile prototypes, frustration, and abandoned projects. This book will help you assess your business idea by subjecting it to pass our seven gates of 'idea killers'. This book introduces you to advanced prompt engineering concepts, enabling you to cross the chasm from being an amateur writing basic prompts to a solo founder shipping secure, low-cost, and scalable applications.

This book is a blueprint for that evolution. It will transform you into an Advanced Prompt Engineer, equipping you with an architectural and software engineering mindset. We will introduce you to a new concept of 'virtual engineering teams' which will provide you, the solo founder with IT departments of your own. We hope this knowledge will help ignite a fast spreading 'fire of innovations' by Solo Founders.

Who will benefit most from this book?

This is a self-help book; it is a practical guide for builders. You do not need to be a senior software engineer to succeed here, but you do need an analytical mindset and familiarity with some core Software Engineering concepts. People with the following backgrounds will benefit most from this book:

- **Developers and Application Architects:** Those who understand systems but want to use AI to improve their productivity or innovate a new product as Solo Founder.

- **Product Managers and QA Testers:** Professionals who understand user flows, edge cases, and testing, they too are ready to invent new products using this book.
- **Tech-Savvy Inventors and Solo Founders:** Entrepreneurs with domain expertise, curious minds who want to build an MVP(Minimum Viable Product) quickly would also benefit from this book. They may need to have perseverance to do some additional self-study to grasp some of the software engineering concepts. Since you no longer need to write code this is a highly viable scenario. Our hope is that this group will be the largest beneficiary of this book.
- **Amateur Programmers and Students:** Those who know the basics of coding and basic prompt engineering, but need a structured methodology to build complex, full-stack web applications. They will benefit from this book, all they will need is to find a viable business idea and it will be like ducks taking to water.

Prompt Engineering

It is the practice of writing clear and concise, while capturing the full scope of the task you are asking the AI chat to accomplish. You can use it to generate a program, analyzing code, generating an image. The focus of this book is to generate production ready code with prompt engineering. Anyone can do it. However, to be able to produce something that is production ready you need to up your game. This book transforms our readers into Advanced Prompt Engineers with the ability to generate working, good quality code. Modern language models can write excellent functions, but software engineering is not just about writing syntax. It is about systems design, state management, security, and integration, quality assurance.

When you rely on basic prompt engineering, you hit a ceiling quickly. Deep in your project you will ask the AI to add a new feature, and it will overwrite a critical database connection. You will ask for a user interface update, and it will forget the authentication rules established 30 prompts ago. This is known as "Architectural Amnesia." Without a structured approach, your application becomes a tangled mess of conflicting logic that is impossible to maintain or deploy.

To build a productionized end-state application at a low cost, you cannot just be a user of AI. You must become the Application Architect. You must define the parameters, isolate the context, and manage the AI just as you would a team of human developers. Only management technique will be different. AI is ready to work with you in the wee hours of night, they don't need breaks or vacations. However, like you need to know your human team members you need to understand the strengths and weaknesses of your AI model.

The old world of software engineering versus the new world

AI has changed the world of coding and software engineering forever. Some of the critical methods and processes from the 'old world' will become unnecessary, these we will have to learn to let go. Some professional developers with many years of coding experience in corporate environments will have the hardest time adjusting to this new post AI world of coding.

In the old world one of the key requirements of writing code was readability by other developers. This concept has been turned on its head in the new paradigm. Now a human developer can take a long complex code file and ask the AI to analyze it. If they know the right questions to ask (good prompt engineering) they will know every twist , turn and security vulnerabilities of that code in less than 5 minutes.

Another example is *code review*. Most companies with big IT departments usually have a 'coding standards policy' that human developers had to follow and another experienced human developer would review: how effective was this process? Not very much. Bugs that are difficult to spot by humans would fall through the cracks like the 'divide by zero' bug. In the new world of AI coding you can confidently automate code review and AI will do a better job applying your standards and auditing it. AI and computers are much better than humans in finding patterns.

That takes us to the next critical component of software engineering- documentation. In the past we produced a lot of design documentation, artifacts that were hallmark of professional programmers and architects and successful projects. We need to carefully review what documentations still make sense in this new world. How those documentations need to change and what new documentations are required for the AI coders.
Being a minimalist person I have identified only a few critical architecture documents for our 'Solo Founder' in this book. These documents I felt were essential for the new world of AI coding.

I have listed architectural and operational documents in Appendix A at the end of this book.

Building in Reality: The SeatSync Project

To learn advanced prompt engineering, you must build something real. Theory alone will not teach you how to navigate a hallucinating AI or deploy a database.
Together, we will build **SeatSync**, a fully functional coffee shop reservation Progressive Web App (PWA). We will start

with a blank folder and end with a live, production-grade application. Throughout this book instead of providing you sample code I will provide you 'prompts' to generate the codes yourself. We will use a modern stack consisting of React and Next.js for the frontend, and backend will be PostgreSQL via Supabase for the database.
By building SeatSync, you will experience the exact challenges of a real-world build. You will learn how to write a Data Logic Contract, how to diagnose code hallucinations, and how to execute a Context Transfer when the AI loses the thread of the application.
The **SeatSync**, is simplified reference architecture intended for educational mapping. It will not survive our seven gates of idea killers. We did not want to waste a real viable business idea for this exercise. However it will take you through the process of building a product quite well which is the main purpose here.

Note 1: I used Vercel, Supabase as infrastructure component for this book. I did not take any money from them nor am I specially inclined to them. I am sure some of you can do this project using Cloudflare Pages, Netlify, Render, Heroku, DigitalOcean App Platform, AWS, Google Cloud, and Microsoft Azure or other service provider. For this project, I selected Vercel and Supabase due to their simplicity and seamless integration.

Meta-Prompting strategy

Throughout this book instead of providing code or install instructions I will encourage you to use prompt engineering to generate all code, installation or configuration instructions. It turns the reading experience into an active prompt engineering workshop. Another advantage is that any installation or configuration instruction provided in this book will be outdated very quickly, however by running the prompt in future you should be getting the latest version of those instructions. So whenever you find yourself struggling with any installation or configuration use our recommended 'The Anatomy of a Perfect Code-Generation Prompt' in chapter 9 and the practices outlined in this book to solve your information need with prompt engineering. I have provided some example prompts in Appendix C and D at the end of this book.

The Roadmap to Production

We will progress through five distinct phases:

- **Part I: The Golden Opportunity** redefines how you view software development and introduces the Isolated Context Methodology.
- **Part II: The Blueprint** covers the foundational architecture and teaches you how to map out the Context Economy before writing a single line of code.
- **Part III: Taming the Machine** addresses the inevitable roadblocks. You will learn advanced techniques to correct AI hallucination, manage memory limits, and inject necessary documentation.
- **Part IV: The Build** is where we execute. We will engineer precise prompts to build out the database, the backend, and the frontend interfaces of SeatSync.
- **Part V: The Launch** focuses on the final mile: automated quality assurance, continuous integration, and deploying your application to the cloud.

You have the idea. Now, it is time to learn the 'how'. Let us begin.

Part I: The Golden Opportunity

Chapter 1: The Golden Age of the Solo Founder

Welcome to the most exciting era in the history of human innovation. For decades, the barrier to entry for building digital products has been high. If you had a brilliant idea for an application, a software platform, or a digital service, you faced a stark choice: spend years learning complex programming languages, or spend tens of thousands of dollars hiring a team of engineers to build it for you. This barrier meant countless world-changing ideas never made it past the notebook phase. They died not because the idea was flawed, but because the visionary lacked the technical capital to execute it.

Today, that barrier has been utterly reduced to a 'bump' in the road. We have entered the Golden Age of the 'Solo Founder'. In this new reality, plain English—or any natural language—has become the most powerful programming language on earth. Generative Artificial Intelligence (AI) has leveled the playing field, granting product innovators, creative thinkers, and domain experts the equivalent of a full engineering department at their fingertips.

Fig 1-1

This chapter will lay the foundation for your journey. We will explore exactly how we arrived at this pivotal moment in technology, uncover the immense power you now wield as a product visionary, and introduce the core design philosophies that will guide every prompt you write. You are no longer just an idea person; you are an architect, a director, and a builder- the Solo Founder.

The Evolution of AI Coding: How We Got Here

To understand the power you hold, you must first understand the journey of the tools you will be using. The timeline of AI code generation is not a slow, linear progression; it is a story of sudden, explosive inflection points. Let us walk through the key moments that transformed the computer from a data processing tool into a creative code developer.

Before 2017: The Brittle Era of Rule-Based AI
Concept: Prior to the modern AI revolution, teaching a computer to code was an exercise in frustration. Early attempts relied on strict, rule-based systems or primitive machine learning models. These systems lacked contextual understanding. If a developer asked an early AI to write a function, the AI would string together code based on rigid templates. It could not understand the 'intent' behind the code, making it practically useless for complex problem-solving. The rule based AI was hitting its architectural limit.

June 2017: The Inflection Point - Transformers

Concept: The world changed quietly in June 2017 when a team of researchers at Google published a scientific paper titled 'Attention Is All You Need'. This paper introduced the Transformer architecture. Before Transformers, AI processed text sequentially, word by word, making it lose track of the beginning of a long sentence by the time it reached the end. The Transformer introduced 'Self-Attention'—a mechanism allowing the model to look at an entire sequence of text at once and understand the relationships between all the words, no matter how far apart they were.
Example: Imagine reading a novel one word at a time through a tiny keyhole, instantly forgetting the previous word. That was AI before 2017. The Transformer kicked the door open, allowing the AI to see the whole page, grasp the context, and understand the narrative. This breakthrough made Large Language Models (LLMs) possible, directly paving the way for AI that could understand the complex, interconnected logic of programming languages.

June 2020: The Arrival of GPT-3

Concept: OpenAI released Generative Pre-trained Transformer 3 (GPT-3). With 175 billion parameters, it was a massive leap forward. While primarily designed for natural language generation, developers quickly realized something astonishing: because GPT-3 was trained on vast swaths of the internet, including public code repositories, it had inadvertently learned how to code. You could prompt it in English to write a simple HTML button or a Python script, and it would generate passable syntax.

Example: A developer went viral by prompting GPT-3 with 'A button that looks like a watermelon' and the AI generated the exact CSS code to create it. This was the spark that ignited the AI coding revolution.

June 2021: GitHub Copilot and the Dawn of Pair Programming

Concept: Recognizing the potential of GPT-3, Microsoft-owned GitHub partnered with OpenAI to create GitHub Copilot. This was a massive inflection point. Copilot was trained specifically on billions of lines of public code from GitHub. It integrated directly into the developer's coding environment, autocompleting lines and entire functions in real-time.

Example: A developer would type a comment like '// function to connect to the database' and Copilot would instantly write the 15 lines of complex syntax required. This proved that AI could drastically speed up professional developers, shifting the mindset from 'AI augments' coders to 'AI replaces coders'.

November 2022: ChatGPT Democratizes Code Generation

Concept: The release of ChatGPT brought conversational AI to the masses. Suddenly, you didn't need to be a developer with a specialized coding environment to use AI. Anyone could open a web browser, type 'Write a Python script to scrape this website,' and receive a fully functional, explained piece of code. This was the moment the door opened for non-technical entrepreneurs. Code generation was no longer locked behind software engineering tools; it was an open dialogue.

2023 to Present: Advanced Reasoning and Large Context Windows

Concept: Models like GPT-4, Claude 3, and Gemini Advanced arrived, bringing advanced reasoning and massive 'context

windows.' Early models could only remember a few pages of text; modern models can process hundreds of pages—or entire software codebases—at once. They don't just write individual functions; they can debug complex systems, suggest architectural improvements, and understand the holistic purpose of your application.
Action Steps: To leverage this history:
Recognize that the AI is not just a search engine; it is a *reasoning engine built on the Transformer architecture.*
Use natural language to explain your intent, not just your technical needs.
Leverage modern context windows by providing the AI with deep background information about your business problem.

Understanding your LLMs Psyche

LLM Psyche is some ways analogous to the human psyche. Understanding this *'LLM Psyche'* will allow you to work with LLMs more effectively.

Memory and childhood experiences: LLMs are trained on a large amount of text data from internet, books, newspapers, any knowledge source available to the platform that trained it. This brings some incorrect and bad data after best efforts to eliminate them by the AI platform. Just as a child going to school may acquire bad habits from peers, an LLM is exposed to the unvetted data and biases of the internet.

Forgetfulness: LLMs generate non-deterministic output. Even if you use the exact same prompt in the same Chat conversation, the model will produce a different response one minute later. It does not "remember" what it said previously for the same prompt. This behavior comes from the underlying architecture of generative models, where randomness — controlled by parameters such as 'temperature' and sampling strategies — influences every token produced.

Because of this inherent random variation, LLMs cannot be relied on for workflows that require exact, repeatable steps. This must be carefully considered when designing solutions, especially in agentic AI systems where deterministic actions are frequently required.

Reasoning: *Large Language Models (LLMs) are hyper-advanced probability engines*. A reasoning engine was added on top. Now LLMs are much smarter when they are allowed to think step-by-step what is known in AI terms as the *'Chain of Thought'*. Break up your problem into smaller chunks whenever possible. LLMs are also natively not very good at Mathematics. Their specialty is language and the next word prediction.

Instincts: LLM platforms are designed to be agreeable to you and your ego. It will not normally be critical of your ideas and will tend to please you. If the probabilistic scope is not defined well in your prompt or is lost during a long conversation the LLM will tend to guess answers from a wider area of its training data which leads to 'hallucinations'. It does not instinctively ask clarifying questions.

Identity/Persona: LLMs work best when you prime your prompt with statements like "You are an elite security expert .... or "You are database architect with 20 years' experience...for our application .. what database will be best? What you are doing by setting the 'identity/persona' is focusing the LLM to look for answers in a certain knowledge domain. This greatly increases its depth and accuracy of the response. It is likely to do less generalization or hallucinations.

Automatic reactions: LLMs love to refactor. To stop this, you must use ***Boundary Forcing***. You tell the AI exactly what it is NOT allowed to touch. This is particularly important when doing AI coding.

Emotional patterns: Be aware of Statistical bias in the training data of the LLMs. Though an AI does not have true emotion at the time of writing this book, it can show statistical bias. While in humans biases can be based on some limited emotional experience, in LLMs the biases are generated by *unbalanced training data*.

Conscious mind: LLMs really do not have any consciousness up to the writing of this book. They are actually a 'Stateless loop' that is reading your whole conversation before generating the response by statistically predicting the next word from a probabilistic space. I think of an LLM as a parrot with vast memory that has learned billions of word tokens and based on your prompt can statistically pick the answer with such high level of 'accuracy' that it seems like the parrot is an Oracle. In reality, like a parrot, it does not have true understanding or commonsense.

AI 'Speak': LLM models do well with certain kind of prompts. These are role playing, relevant information dense, void of unnecessary information, with clear instructions of what to do, what not to do and minimum conversational 'fluff'.

Lying during hallucinations: Although LLMs generally produce high accuracy outputs, a model operating outside its active context window will generate fabricated specifications or non-existent code libraries without technical warnings. While this effectively equates to lying in human conversations, the machine executes this without malice; it is merely predicting statistically plausible tokens within an unconstrained probability space. It is just trying to do its job within the architectural framework of an LLM. There is a known incident where an AI-generated legal brief contained a fictitious case reference. It is critical to understand hallucinations to use AI effectively. Later in this book we will deep dive in this topic.

Contemplate and ground yourself in this knowledge about LLMs before proceeding.

The Golden Opportunity: Power of an Engineering Department

We are experiencing a fundamental shift in the economics of product development. Historically, the value in software creation was held by those who knew the syntax—the human compilers who translated business requirements into machine code. Today, the AI handles the syntax. The value has shifted from 'knowing how to code' to 'knowing what to build.' Concept: This is your Golden Opportunity. If you are a product innovator, an amateur coder, or a tech savvy creative visionary, you understand software engineering concepts or you are curious and can acquire the knowledge needed, you possess the domain expertise. A point to note you don't need to be able to write code, you just need to understand the various concepts and disciplines of software engineering. You understand the customer, the market gap, and the business logic. AI allows you to bypass the technical middleman. You now have the power of a front-end developer, a back-end engineer, a database architect, and a quality assurance tester or an Application Security Engineer, only a prompt away.

Fig 1-2

Consider this scene: A logistics manager who noticed a massive inefficiency in how their company routed delivery trucks. The manager had no formal coding background. In 2019, he would have needed $50,000 to hire an agency to build a prototype. Instead, using advanced prompt engineering, he treated the AI as his CTO. He dictated the business logic, asked the AI to recommend a tech stack, and step-by-step prompted the generation of a web application. In six weeks, working evenings, he built a functional, deployable SaaS product that he later sold back to his own industry.

Contemplate these action steps:

You are a product inventor and a technical founder. You are now a systems architect.

Focus your energy on deeply understanding your user's problem;

Work with AI and develop your technical architecture.

Let the AI handle the mechanical building of the solution.

Embrace iterative building (Build a small piece → test it → fix it → improve it → add the next piece → repeat). You are the director, guiding the AI to refine its output step-by-step.
You will become an 'Advanced prompt Engineer', an artist of prompt engineering. This book will guide you step by step in that journey.

Introducing the Core Philosophy

With power comes the necessity for discipline. AI can write code instantly, but it can also write bad, overly complex, and insecure code instantly. Because you are orchestrating the build, you must enforce a strict set of design principles. Throughout this book, we will embed the following six core philosophies into every prompt and architectural decision you make.

1. Simplicity

Concept: Complexity is the vulnerability of any system. AI and humans tend to over-engineer solutions if left unchecked. A simple solution is actually a work of art. A simple, well-understood architecture is vastly superior to a complex, cutting-edge architecture that you cannot maintain.
Example: If you need to store user data, the AI might suggest a complex microservices architecture with a distributed NoSQL database. While powerful, it's unnecessary for an MVP (Minimum Viable Product).
Action Steps:
Always prompt the AI to 'provide the simplest, most maintainable solution.'
Reject code that you cannot fundamentally understand when the AI explains it to you.

2. Security

Concept: Amateur coders often leave security as an afterthought. As a prompt engineer, you must build security into the foundation. AI is trained on public code, which includes publicly available security flaws. You must explicitly instruct it to follow secure coding practices.
Action Steps:
Include security constraints in your base prompts (e.g., 'Ensure all user inputs are sanitized to prevent SQL injection').
Have a dedicated AI session act as a 'Virtual Security Auditor' to review your generated code before deployment.

3. Privacy
Concept: In the modern digital landscape, data privacy is non-negotiable. Designing for privacy means collecting only the data you absolutely need and ensuring it is stored safely and safe in transit.

Action Steps:
Prompt your virtual database architecture team(an AI chat, more on this later) to minimize personal data collection.
Ask the AI to implement data encryption at rest and in transit from day one.

4. Scalability
Concept: While we prioritize simplicity, we must not paint ourselves into a corner. Scalability means building a simple foundation that can handle success (growth) without requiring a complete rewrite.
Example: Hardcoding file paths or database URLs directly into your application code makes scaling impossible. Using environment variables from the start makes scaling to the cloud seamless.
Action Steps:
Ask the AI to decouple your front-end from your back-end (e.g., using APIs).
In design discussions with AI prompt for code that is modular, so pieces can be upgraded independently later.

5. Prompt Token and Context Memory Optimization
Concept: This is the most crucial skill you will learn from this book. AI models have a 'context window'—a limit to how much conversation they can remember. No matter which AI platform you may be using: Anthropic, Gemini, ChatGPT, Grok they are all bound by this architectural limit. Every word you type and every line of code the AI generates consumes 'tokens.' If you clutter the chat, the AI will 'forget' your earlier instructions and start hallucinating.
Action Steps:
Keep your prompts concise and strictly relevant to the current task. If needed, open a parallel chat session in a separate window with a different AI platform for asking clarifying questions parallel to your main AI coding chat.
Do not dump entire codebases into the chat unless necessary; provide only the relevant snippets.
Regularly ask the AI to summarize the current state of the project, then use that summary to start a fresh, uncluttered chat session. More on this topic in later chapters.

6. Low-Cost / Low-Energy Approach
Concept: A solo founder must protect their runway. AI allows you to build incredibly lean systems that cost pennies to run. You should actively design your architecture to utilize serverless functions, managed databases with generous free tiers, and optimized code so it doesn't waste computational power. Remember high computation means high energy use and that means harming the environment somewhere.

Action Steps:
Prompt your 'Virtual AI architecture team' to select infrastructure that scales down to zero cost when not in use.
Ask the AI to optimize database queries to reduce processing time which reduces energy consumption.
By internalizing these six principles, you elevate yourself from someone who merely generates code snippets to an entrepreneur who architects sustainable, production-ready software. In the next chapter, we will take your raw business idea and use AI to transform it into a rigorous, validated

proposition ready for development. Your virtual AI team is waiting. Let's get to work.

Chapter 2: From Problem to Proposition: Validating Your Idea

In the previous chapter, we established a new reality: the technical barrier to building software has fallen. With Generative AI as your Chief Technology Officer, you now possess the execution capabilities of an entire engineering department. However, this newfound power introduces a dangerous new trap for the solo founder. When building software that costs practically nothing in terms of capital and takes only weeks instead of months, the temptation is to build simply because you can.

This is the 'Builder's Fallacy.' Many amateur coders and early-stage entrepreneurs rush to prompt their AI to write code for the first idea that pops into their heads. They spend weeks meticulously crafting user interfaces and database architectures for a product that nobody actually wants. The ability to build rapidly does not negate the fundamental laws of business. A perfectly engineered application that solves a nonexistent problem is still a failure. In fact, building without validation is the fastest way to exhaust your mental energy, and ultimately abandon your entrepreneurial journey.

This chapter is about restraint and validation. Before you assign a single coding task to your AI virtual teams, you should ensure your business idea is a diamond worth cutting. We will explore how to identify everyday problems and transform them into compelling business propositions. We will then turn your AI into a world-class research analyst to assess your value proposition and dissect your competition.
Finally, drawing from the most sophisticated entrepreneurial research from institutions like Harvard Business School, Stanford, and Wharton, we will introduce a novel framework: The ***Seven Gates of the Idea Killers***. This is a gauntlet designed to stress-test your idea. If your concept survives these seven gates, it is ready for the development phase.

Finding the Spark: Transforming Everyday Problems into Ideas

Concept: The best business ideas rarely come from brainstorming sessions in a vacuum. They are born from observation. Remember the idiom 'necessity is the mother of invention'. Good ideas emerge from the friction, annoyance, and inefficiencies of everyday life and professional work. As an entrepreneur, your primary job is to become an expert observer of pain points preferably in your domain of experience.
A problem only becomes a business idea when you can identify a scalable way to solve it for a specific group of people who are willing to pay for the solution. The transformation from 'complaint' to 'company' requires structuring the problem into a clear Value Proposition—a statement that explains what benefit you provide, who you provide it for, and how you do it uniquely well.

Example: Consider the origin of the ride-sharing industry. The problem was simple: standing in the rain trying to hail a taxi in a busy city was incredibly frustrating, and calling a dispatch company was unreliable. The founders did not start by saying, 'Let's build a global logistics platform.' They started with the everyday problem. The transformation into a business idea was recognizing that everyone had a GPS-enabled supercomputer in their pocket, creating a mechanism to match supply (idle drivers) with demand (stranded passengers). Then they were able execute on their idea as they had the resources. I am painfully aware of someone who saw the same problem two years earlier but was not able to execute due to the technical/financial barrier of those days.

Action Steps for Identifying Problems:
The Friction Audit: For one week, carry a small notebook or use a notes app on your phone. Write down every time you say or you hear someone say , 'I hate doing this,' 'This takes

too long,' or 'Why isn't there a better way to do this?' or 'Why do I have to go to that expert to get what I need'?

The Domain Deep Dive: Look closely at your own profession and your daily life. What is the most tedious, repetitive task that you and your colleagues despise? Enterprise software built by domain experts (you) is vastly superior to software built by outsiders guessing at the problem. In the old world of software engineering there was a hilarious illustration of a customer asking to build a swing and the requirements were developed by a project manager who explained to the developer. When the customer came to see the product, the swing was unusable. It was a funny reality.

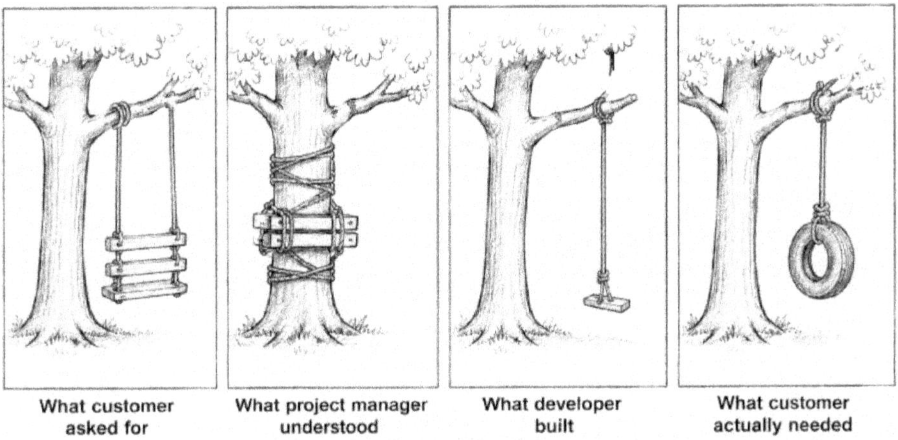

Fig 2-1

Imagine this scenario in our new world of AI coding: for the Solo Founder, this problem never even arises. The 'customer' , the project manager and the developer are the same person. Imagine the stride in efficiency.
I digress. Let's get back to our topic.

The 'Follow the Spreadsheet' Rule: If you see people managing a complex process using a massively convoluted Microsoft Excel spreadsheet, there is almost always a SaaS (Software as a Service) business idea waiting to be built to replace it.

Or if a service is very expensive can you replace that with a new cheaper Web Application.

AI as Your Research Analyst: Value Proposition and Competitors

Once you have identified a problem and brainstormed a potential solution, you must assess its viability. Traditionally, this required expensive market research firms or weeks of tedious Google searches. Today, your AI platform is your Chief Strategy Officer.
However, you must use AI correctly. Do not ask the AI, 'Is my idea good?' The AI is designed to be helpful and conversational; it will naturally lean towards validating your ego and telling you it is a brilliant concept. Instead, you must prompt the AI to be critical, objective, and data-driven.

Prompting for Value Proposition Assessment
To assess your value proposition, you want the AI to play the role of a skeptical target customer and an expert business strategist.

Example Prompt: *'Act as a seasoned venture capitalist and a skeptical target customer. My business idea is [*INSERT IDEA: E.G., A MOBILE APP THAT USES AI TO ANALYZE A USER'S REFRIGERATOR CONTENTS AND GENERATES WEEKLY MEAL PLANS TO REDUCE FOOD WASTE*]. Identify the top three reasons why customers would refuse to use this product. What is the actual underlying 'job' they are trying to get done? How does my idea fail to address that job smoothly?'*

Prompting for Competitive Analysis
Do not assume you have no competitors. If you truly have no competitors, it often means there is no market. Competitors validate that the problem exists. You want to use AI to find direct competitors, indirect competitors, and the dreaded

'status quo' (what people are doing right now instead of using your proposed solution).

Example Prompt: *'Conduct a competitive analysis for my proposed business: [*INSERT IDEA*]. Identify 3 direct competitors and 3 indirect competitors. For each, list their core value proposition, their primary weakness (read negative user reviews if you have access to web search data), and their pricing model. Finally, explain what the 'status quo' alternative is. How do people solve this problem today without buying any software?'*

Action Steps:
Run these prompts in your chosen AI platform (like ChatGPT Plus, Claude 3, or Gemini Advanced, or you.com).
Pay special attention to the 'status quo.' Your biggest competitor is rarely another startup; it is usually human habit and inertia.
Refine your value proposition based on the AI's critique. If the AI points out a fatal flaw, adjust the idea before moving to the next stage.
Run your ideas by some people who are affected by the problem.
Let go of any poor or bad ideas and move on.

The Academic Foundation: Consider following concepts that will help you screen your own ideas.

To build a truly robust validation process, we must look beyond startup blogs and tap into the rigorous academic research of the world's leading business schools. The framework we are about to introduce synthesizes three critical academic concepts:

1. The 'Jobs to be Done' Theory (Harvard Business School): Pioneered by the late Clayton Christensen, this theory posits

that people do not simply buy products; they 'hire' them to make progress in specific circumstances. You must validate that your idea fulfills a high-priority, poorly satisfied need.
Reference: Clayton Christensen's landmark book, 'Competing Against Luck' (2016)
2. The Lean Startup Methodology (Stanford Influence): Steve Blank and Eric Ries popularized the concept of 'Customer Development' and the Minimum Viable Product. The core academic takeaway is that a startup is not a smaller version of a large company; it is a temporary organization designed to search for a repeatable and scalable business model under conditions of extreme uncertainty.
Reference: Ries, E. (2011). The Lean Startup: How Today's Entrepreneurs Use Continuous Innovation to Create Radically Successful Businesses. Built on the Customer Development framework introduced by Steve Blank in The Four Steps to the Epiphany (2003).
3. The VRIO Framework (Strategic Management, Wharton/Barney): To have a sustainable business, your solution must be Valuable, Rare, Inimitable (hard to copy), and Organized to capture value. This ensures you aren't just building a feature that a larger company can instantly copy.
Reference: Barney, Jay. "Firm Resources and Sustained Competitive Advantage." Journal of Management 17, no. 1 (1991): 99–120.

By combining these academic pillars with our core philosophies of Simplicity, Scalability, and Low-Cost execution, we arrive at the ultimate stress test for the AI-augmented entrepreneur our version of the 'Shark Tank' which we are calling ' Passing the gates of seven Idea Killers'.

The Seven Gates of the Idea Killer

Fig 2-2

Welcome to the mountain pass where you will have to pass 'Seven Gates of the Idea Killers'. The purpose of this process is to kill weak ideas quickly so you do not waste your time and AI tokens building them. You must brutally force your business concept by passing by each of these 'idea killers'. If your idea gets killed , you must either pivot the idea until it passes, or abandon it entirely. Let go of your creative emotion for this phase of the journey.

Gate 1: Are you building a painkiller or a vitamin (The Problem Focus)

Concept: This gate tests whether you are building a 'painkiller' or a 'vitamin'. Vitamins are nice to have; painkillers are essential. Does the customer recognize they have a problem, and is it painful enough that they are actively seeking a solution? If the customer doesn't know they have a problem, you will go bankrupt trying to educate them.

The Killer Question: 'What specific, painful task is the customer trying to accomplish, and what highly frustrating workaround are they currently using?'
How to pass: You must be able to document the exact, painful workaround the customer currently uses. If they aren't currently trying to solve the problem (even poorly), the pain isn't acute enough.

Gate 2: Will anyone pay? (The Value Proposition)
Concept: It is easy to find people who will say your idea is cool. It is incredibly difficult to find people who will give you their credit card. What is the economic reality of the customer? Are they willing to pay, and are they capable of paying?
The Killer Question: 'Is the target customer willing to part with actual money to solve this problem, and do they have the authority to make the purchase?'
How to pass: You must identify a clear monetization model. If your plan is 'we will give it away for free and monetize with ads later,' you fail this gate. As a solo founder, you need unit economics that make sense from day one. You must validate that the cost of the problem is significantly higher than the price you will charge for the solution.

Gate 3: The Moat (Competitive Advantage)
Concept: This gate applies the VRIO (Value, Rarity, Imitability, and Organization) framework. Because AI makes it so easy to build software, the barrier to entry is very low. If you build a simple habit-tracking app, 1,000 other people can use AI to build the exact same app tomorrow. You should have a 'moat'—a defense against imitation.
The Killer Question: 'Once I launch this, what prevents a larger company or another AI-enabled entrepreneur from copying it in a weekend?'
How to pass: Your moat cannot simply be 'I built it first.' Passable moats include: proprietary data that only you possess, deep domain expertise that allows you to design a superior workflow, an established audience or distribution

channel you already control, or a deeply integrated community.

Gate 4: Simplicity and size
Concept: As a solo founder orchestrating AI, you cannot build the next Facebook or a massive multiplayer online game as your first project. The architecture required is too complex, project size is too big for a 'solo founder'.
The Killer Question: 'Can the core value of this idea be delivered with a simple, three-tier architecture (Front-end, Back-end API, Simple Database) without requiring complex machine learning algorithms, real-time physics engines, or massive hardware integrations?'
How to pass: If the idea requires you to invent new technology, hardware, or manage thousands of concurrent real-time WebSocket connections, it fails this Gate. Keep it simple.

Gate 5: Market size and scaling (Market Dynamics)
Concept: This gate evaluates whether the juice is worth the squeeze. Is the market large enough to support a viable business, and does the software scale naturally? Some problems are very painful, but only affect 100 people in the world.
The Killer Question: 'How big is my market? Can I serve my 10,000th customer with almost the same effort and cost as my 10th customer?'
How to pass: The market must be big enough to generate sufficient revenue. The business must be fundamentally software-driven. If every new customer requires you to perform hours of manual consulting work, you do not have a software business; you have a consulting firm. To pass, the cost of adding an additional user (marginal cost) must be close to zero.
Gate 6: Cost of the first customer
Concept: This gate enforces our Low-Cost/Low-Energy philosophy. Solo founders fail when they run out of money or patience. If your idea requires you to train a massive, custom

AI model from scratch costing $50,000 in server time before you get your first customer, you will probably fail.
The Killer Question: 'Can I build and host the Minimum Viable Product (MVP) of this idea for less than $50-100 a month using serverless infrastructure and API integrations?'
How to pass: You must design the system to use existing tools. Instead of building an email server, you use the SendGrid API. Instead of training an AI model, you use the OpenAI or Gemini API. You pass this gate by proving the idea can be built cheaply by gluing together existing services.

Gate 7: Are you passionate about the product?
Concept: This is the most personal and often most difficult gate. Building a business is a grind. Even with AI writing the code, marketing, supporting customers, and iterating the product will test your resilience. If you do not care about the problem or the people experiencing it, you will quit when things get hard.
The Killer Question: 'Do I have a unique passion, unfair advantage, or deep background in this specific industry that will sustain me when the going gets tough?'
How to pass: You must honestly assess your connection to the problem. If you are a dentist building software for dental clinics, you pass easily. If you are a dentist trying to build software for long-haul truck drivers because 'the market looks lucrative,' you fail. Stick to what you know or what you deeply love.

Case Study: Passing the Gates

To understand how to apply this framework, let's look at a real-world example of an incredibly successful solo-founder style business that would have perfectly passed the Seven Gates: Calendly.

Story: Before Calendly, the process of scheduling a business meeting was a nightmare of email ping-pong. 'Does Tuesday at 2 PM work?' 'No, how about Wednesday at 4 PM?' 'I'm in a

different time zone, is that EST or PST?' Tope Awotona, the founder, recognized this immense friction.
Let us run the core concept of Calendly through our Seven Gates of the Idea Killer:
Gate 1: Are you building a painkiller or a vitamin . The job was clear: 'Schedule a meeting with another human being without exchanging 5 emails.' The workaround was painful and universally recognized.
Gate 2: Will anyone pay? (The Value Proposition). Sales professionals, recruiters, and consultants lose money when meetings don't happen. They are highly motivated to pay $10/month for a tool that makes them look professional and secures the meeting.
Gate 3: The Moat (Competitive Advantage). Initially, the moat was weak (it's just a calendar integration). However, Calendly built a 'viral loop' moat. Every time a user sent a Calendly link to a client, the client experienced the product. The product marketed itself, creating an insurmountable distribution advantage.
Gate 4: Simplicity and size. The architecture is elegantly simple. It requires a front-end UI, a database to store user preferences, and API connections to Google Calendar and Outlook. It perfectly aligns with the capabilities of AI generation.
Gate 5: Market size and scaling (Market Dynamics). Once the code is written, serving 1 million users costs marginally more in software development and infrastructure than serving 100 users. It is pure software scale.
Gate 6: Cost of the first customer. The MVP could absolutely be built using low-cost cloud hosting and standard web frameworks. It relies heavily on existing infrastructure (Google's calendar data) rather than generating its own heavy data.
Gate 7: Are you passionate about the product? Awotona was a sales representative who personally felt the intense pain of losing deals due to scheduling friction. He had deep empathy for the target user.
Calendly is a masterpiece of simple, highly validated problem solving.

Contrast this with a failed idea like Quibi, which raised nearly $2 billion to create short-form premium video for mobile phones. Quibi failed Gate 1 (people already had YouTube and TikTok for short-form mobile video; there was no painful unmet need) and failed Gate 4 (it required massive, complex Hollywood studio integration). They built it because they could, not because it passed any gates.

Conclusion and Next Steps

Do not skip this validation process. Your AI virtual teams are waiting patiently to build whatever you command, but they are completely blind to market realities. They cannot tell you if your idea is economically viable; they can only generate the code for it.

By forcing your ideas through the Seven Gates of the Idea Killers, you filter out the noise. You protect your time, your energy, and your capital. When an idea finally survives all seven gates, you will move forward with confidence, knowing you are building a solution that the market actually wants.

Even after diligence your idea may fail. No gate can protect you from reality. But don't stay on the ground; get up and try again and cherish your failure. I agree with Jeff Bezos on his statement 'failure and invention are inseparable twins' (*originates from Jeff Bezos' 2016 Amazon shareholder letter*). Netflix's culture memo says 'you admit mistakes openly and share learnings widely' (*Netflix. (2024). Netflix Culture Memo: Seeking Excellence. Netflix, Inc.* https://jobs.netflix.com/culture). As a 'Solo Founder', entrepreneur be willing to risk failure in pursuit of success, cherish the learning from failure.

In the next chapter, we will take your validated business idea and begin the practical work. We will introduce you to a novel idea of a new type of teams: the specialized AI virtual engineering team. We will learn how to structure them, how to feed them your validated concept, and how to begin architecting a simple, scalable solution.

Part II: The Blueprint – Architecture and Virtual Teams

Chapter 3: Redefining the "Development Team"

Congratulations. By passing your business concept through the Seven Gates of the Idea Killers in the previous chapter, you have accomplished something most amateur founders never do: you have validated your idea against economic and practical reality. You are no longer acting on a whim. You hold a viable, stress-tested business proposition.

Now, we face the chasm between idea and reality. Historically, this is where the solo founder was forced to hand over their vision to a team of human software engineers. We have seen this handover fail countless times. Miscommunications, misaligned incentives, and organizational chaos frequently warp a brilliant idea into a bloated, unusable product. See figure 2-1 in last chapter.

In the age of Generative AI, you do not have to hire an agency. But you still need an engineering organization. If you simply open a single AI chat window and type, "Build me my app," you will create a disaster. Software engineering has fundamental laws that apply whether humans or machines are writing the syntax. The most famous is Conway's Law, which states that software structures will inevitably mirror the communication structures of the organization that built them. If your organization is a single, massive, chaotic AI chat log where you discuss database architecture, marketing copy, and button colors in the same breath, your resulting software will be a chaotic, tangled mess. The AI will lose context, hallucinate, and eventually collapse under the weight of its own confused memory.

In this chapter, we will redefine the "Development Team." We are going to borrow the most battle-tested principles of traditional software engineering—modularity, separation of concerns, and clear documentation—and adapt them for the AI era. We will build a streamlined, highly disciplined virtual organization. *Your new development team will consist of specialized, strictly segregated AI chat conversations*. This is a totally new software engineering concept from us for the 'solo founder' in the new world of AI generated coding. It will enable you to manage the technical challenges of AI assisted coding and organize your project management, increasing the probability of success significantly.

The Running Example: Introducing SeatSync

To make these abstract engineering concepts practical, we will build a product together throughout this book. Let us imagine you have passed the following idea through our Seven Gates:

The Problem: Remote workers often struggle to find reliable seating and power outlets at local coffee shops. Meanwhile, coffee shop owners struggle with low revenue during mid-afternoon off-peak hours.

Note 2*: The problem is not something we are claiming to be original nor something that will actually pass our 'Seven gates of the idea killer' which we proposed. We are using this as simple example for the rest of the book to teach our process and methods.*

The Proposition (SeatSync): A simple web application that allows remote workers to reserve a guaranteed table at local coffee shops during off-peak hours for a small fee, which includes unlimited drip coffee.

SeatSync is economically viable, operationally simple, and easily scalable. It perfectly embodies our core philosophies. Now, let us organize the teams that will build it.

The Paradigm Shift: A Team is a dedicated Chat Tab

Fig 3-1

Concept: In the new frontier of AI-powered product development, a "team" is no longer a group of human beings in a room. A team is a dedicated, isolated chat conversation with your AI platform.

Why must we isolate them? Because of the concept of the "Context Window"—the AI's active memory limit. If you ask an AI to write a complex database query, and earlier in that exact same conversation you were brainstorming 50 different color palettes for the marketing website, the AI's attention is diluted. It has to process the color palettes while trying to reason through data logic. This is when the AI "forgets" your strict security rules or hallucinates non-existent code libraries.

By keeping teams segregated into distinct chat threads, you ensure 100% pure focus. The Database Team never hears about the Marketing Team's problems. The Front-end Team doesn't care how the deployment pipeline is configured. This is called "Separation of Concerns," and it is the bedrock of robust software engineering. We are adopting this to the new world of AI assisted coding.

Structuring Your Virtual Enterprise

For a project like SeatSync, we will establish five distinct virtual teams. Each team represents a new, fresh chat window. Do not open them all at once; you will interact with them sequentially and in parallel as the project demands.

1. The Architecture / Design Team

Scope of Work: This is your lead engineering group. You will use this chat to brainstorm the technical stack, establish data flows, and make the highest-level decisions. This team writes NO production code. Its only job is to create the design documents that the other teams will follow.

2. Back-End & DB Team

Scope of Work: Responsible for how data is structured and stored. For SeatSync, this team will design the tables for Users, Coffee Shops, and Reservations. They will generate the SQL scripts or NoSQL schemas required to build the database securely and efficiently. Generates any needed Edge Functions. This team cares about logic, speed, and security.

3. The Front-end Team

Scope of Work: Everything the user sees and clicks. This chat will generate the HTML, CSS, React, or mobile app code. They care about user experience (UX), responsive design (making it look good on mobile and desktop), and accessibility.

4. The DevOps / Infrastructure Team

Scope of Work: Where the code lives. This chat helps you select the cloud provider (like AWS, Vercel, or Heroku), sets up your domain name, configures your servers, and writes the scripts that move your code from your laptop to the public internet securely.

5. The Product Marketing Team
Scope of Work: The growth engine. This chat is entirely divorced from the code. It is responsible for crafting the landing page copy, writing launch emails, optimizing SEO (Search Engine Optimization), and brainstorming go-to-market strategies to acquire SeatSync's first 100 users.

The AI-Software Engineering Methodology
In traditional software engineering, we relied on massive, 100-page documents called Business Requirements Documents (BRDs) or Software Requirements Specifications (SRS). We used complex UML diagrams to map out every interaction. The key purpose was to maintain coding standards and share the knowledge with developers and other present and future team members. Historically a developer would need days of reading and testing the code to be able to take over support or updating the code. In the new world of AI assisted coding you paste a piece of code in a chat window and ask the engine to explain the code, functions , input outputs and you get a better than human analysis in matter seconds or minutes.
In the AI era, this heavy documentation is actually counterproductive. If you feed an AI a 100-page document, it will struggle to weigh which parts are most important. We need a simpler methodology. I am calling this the *"Isolated Context Methodology"* (ICM).
ICM relies on a minimalist documentation suite. We will keep the best of standard software engineering from the old world —clear contracts between systems—without the bloat. We will rely on just three core design documents and one critical maintenance document. These documents act as the connective tissue between your isolated AI chat tabs.

Document 1: The Core Blueprint (The Common Shared Document)
Concept: The Core Blueprint is the single source of truth for the entire project. It contains no actual code. It is a high-level summary that you will paste into the very first prompt of every new virtual team you spin up. It transfers an architectural

summary of the project into the AI's context window immediately.
Purpose: To align all teams on what we are building, who we are building it for, and our core philosophical constraints.

Contents:
Project Name & short Summary. Take your time developing this document. Personally I sometimes take days writing a one page document. You have to choose your words precisely without losing important context.
Target Audience (e.g., Remote workers, independent coffee shop owners).
Core Features (No more than 3-4 features for the MVP).
The Tech Stack (e.g., React frontend, Node.js backend, PostgreSQL database).
Strict Constraints (e.g., "Must be low-cost serverless hosting," "Must prioritize mobile-first UI," "Must sanitize all inputs for security").

Document 2: The Data Logic Contract
Concept: This is generated by the Architecture Team and shared with the Database and Back-end teams. It simply lists exactly what data we are collecting and how the system interacts with it.
Purpose: To prevent the Front-end team from asking for a "User's Favorite Drink" if the Database team never built a place to store it.
Contents:
Entities (User, Shop, Reservation).
Attributes (User has Name, Email, Password Hash).

Document 3: The Interface Contract
Concept: This is shared between the Design Team, Front-end Team, and Marketing Team. It dictates the look, feel, and user journey.
Purpose: To ensure visual consistency and a smooth user experience without bogging down the database teams with color hex codes.
Contents:
Brand Colors and Typography.
User Flow (Step 1: Login -> Step 2: View Map -> Step 3: Book Seat).
Key UI components needed (Navigation bar, Map view, Checkout modal).

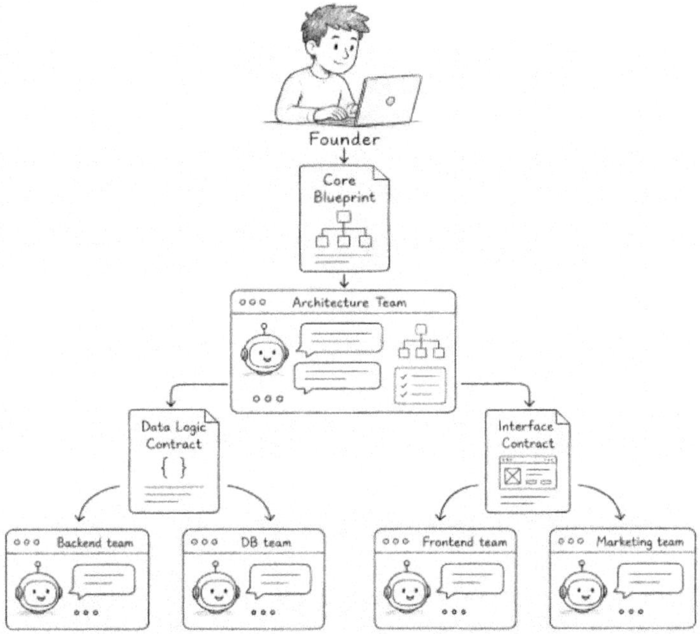

Fig 3-2

Step-by-Step: From Idea to Implementation Plan

Now that we understand the structure, let us put the methodology into practice. We are going to open our first AI chat tab—the Architecture / Design Team—and prompt it to help us build our Core Blueprint and our implementation plan.

Step 1: Bootstrapping the Architecture Team

Action Steps: Open a brand new, empty chat session with your AI platform. Your first prompt must set the persona and establish the baseline.

Example Prompt: "*Act as a Principal Software Architect with 20 years of experience building lean, highly scalable SaaS platforms. We are going to build a web application called SeatSync. The goal is to allow remote workers to book off-peak tables at local coffee shops. Our core design philosophies are Simplicity, Security, Privacy, Scalability, and Low-Cost execution. Ask me 5 clarifying questions about the business logic before we decide on a technology stack.*"

Why this works: You are assigning a highly competent persona. You are injecting your core philosophies immediately. By asking the AI to ask YOU questions, you force a collaborative design process rather than letting the AI blindly guess what you want.

Step 2: Defining the Tech Stack

Action Steps: Answer the AI's questions. Then, prompt it to select the most efficient tools.

Example Prompt: "*Based on our discussion, recommend a modern, simple tech stack for SeatSync. We need a frontend framework, a backend language (if absolutely necessary on technical ground), a database, and a cloud hosting provider. Prioritize tools that are cheap to start, have massive community support (so you, the AI, know how to write code for*

them easily), and are highly secure. Provide a brief justification for each choice."
The AI might recommend: React (Frontend), Node.js with Express (Backend), Supabase or PostgreSQL (Database), and Vercel or Heroku (Hosting). Approve these choices if it agrees with your own research. Choose the simplest solution.

Step 3: Generating the Core Blueprint

Action Steps: Now that the architecture is decided, command the AI to generate the first of our three minimalist design documents.
Example Prompt: "*Excellent. Now, generate our 'Core Blueprint'. This will be a short, highly structured document that I will share with other specialized AI development teams to give them context. It must include the Project Summary, Target Audience, 3-4 Core MVP Features, our chosen Tech Stack, and our strict philosophical constraints. Keep it under 500 words and format it clearly.*"

You now save this generated output into a physical Word or text document on your computer. This is your master key.

Step 4: Generating the Domain Contracts
Action Steps: Stay in the Architecture chat. Ask it to map out the technical specifics.

Example Prompt: "*Now, act as a Systems Analyst. Generate the 'Data Logic Contract' for SeatSync. Give me a simple bulleted list of the database entities (like User, Shop, Reservation) and their core fields. Then list the 5 most important functions we will need (e.g., user login, create reservation). Keep it simple, avoiding overly complex relational mapping for now.*"

Save this output to your computer.

Orchestrating the Teams: How to Avoid Crossing Streams

You now have your documents. How do you actually use them without confusing the AI? This requires discipline from you, the sole founder.
Rule 1: The Blueprint Introduction.
Whenever you open a new chat tab (for example, the Database Team), your very first prompt must be:

"*You are the Database Engineering Team. I am your technical founder. We are building a product. Here is the Core Blueprint for context: [Paste Blueprint]. Your sole focus is database design. Acknowledge that you understand your role.*"

Rule 2: Stay in your lane.
If you are in the Front-end chat building the reservation button, and you realize you need a new database field to store the time of the reservation, DO NOT ask the Front-end chat to write the database code.
Instead, follow this flow:

1. Go to the Database chat tab.
2. Example Prompt: "*We need to add a 'Time' field to the Reservation table. Please provide the SQL command to update the schema.*"
3. Update your 'Data Logic Contract' document on your computer.
4. Go back to the Front-end chat tab. Prompt: "*The backend now accepts a 'Time' field. Update the UI to include a time-picker dropdown and reservation function to accept and save this field.*"

This seems tedious at first. Why jump between three tabs when one AI could write it all? Because if you let one AI tab do it all, by week three of your project, the AI will completely lose track of how the database connects to the frontend. It will overwrite code, invent phantom bugs, and you will spend days untangling the mess. The Isolated Context Methodology protects the AI from its own memory limits.

The Product Marketing Team: Building While Coding

Software engineering is not just about code; it is about delivering a product to a market. Do not wait until the app is finished to start marketing. You should spin up your Product Marketing Team chat immediately after generating the Core Blueprint.

Provide this team with the Core Blueprint and the Interface Contract. Their job is not to write loops or variables, but to translate the technical reality into human value.

Example Prompt for Marketing Team: "*You are the Chief Marketing Officer for SeatSync. Read the attached Core Blueprint. Our objective this week is to build a waitlist of 500 remote workers and 20 coffee shop owners in our city. Design a 3-step email campaign targeting coffee shop owners, explaining the value proposition of monetizing their empty seats without confusing them with technical jargon.*"

By running the Marketing team in parallel with your coding teams, you ensure that the product you are engineering matches the story you are telling the market.

Conclusion: Discipline over Speed

AI has made coding incredibly fast. But speed without direction is a car crash. By redefining your development team into highly focused, strictly isolated AI chat sessions, and anchoring them with three simple, shared design documents, you install guardrails on the highway.

You have successfully transitioned from an idea person to a Systems Architect. You have your Core Blueprint, your Data Contracts, and your virtual teams are standing by. In the next chapter, we will open those tabs and begin the deep architectural work, diving into the specifics of selecting and configuring your simple, scalable technical stack.

Chapter 4: Architecting for Simplicity and Scale

Welcome to the most critical conversation you will have in your journey as a Solo Founder. You have rigorously validated your idea through our 'Seven Gates of the Idea Killers'. You have defined your problem, verified your audience's willingness to pay, and mapped out a simple, friction-free Core Blueprint. Now, it is time to complete architectural and engineering artifacts.

But before a single line of code is written, we must design the blueprint of the house. We need to decide what materials to use, how the plumbing will connect to the grid, and ensure the foundation will not crack when the second floor is added. In the traditional software world, this is the domain of the Systems Architect or the Chief Technology Officer (CTO).
In our new paradigm, this is the domain of your Architecture Virtual Team.
This chapter will teach you how to conduct highly effective design discussions with your Architecture AI Chat. We will explore how to select the right stack, pick the most AI-friendly programming languages, and choose a database that balances your current needs with future scale. Most importantly, every decision we make will be heavily filtered through our core philosophies: Simplicity, Security, Privacy, Scalability, Context Memory Optimization, and Low-Cost infrastructure.

The AI Architecture Discussion: Talking to Your Virtual CTO

When speaking to the Architecture AI team, adopt the persona of a visionary Product Owner talking to a highly experienced, somewhat pragmatic Senior Engineer. Your goal is not to dictate the technology; your goal is to present the business constraints and the Core Blueprint, and let the AI propose the optimal technical path.

The biggest mistake founders make at this stage is walking into the AI chat and saying, "Write a React Native app that does X,Y, Z." By pre-selecting the technology, you bypass the AI's greatest strength: its ability to synthesize millions of architectural patterns to find the path of least resistance for your specific problem.

Instead, we use the Isolated Context Methodology (ICM). We provide the AI with our Core Blueprint, and we establish strict boundaries.

Concept: The Constraints Prompt

To get the best architectural advice, you must prime the AI with your core philosophies. You are defining the rules of the game before the AI makes its first move. This minimizes token waste and keeps the AI from hallucinating complex, over-engineered enterprise solutions that you cannot afford to host.

Example: Priming the Architecture AI Team

Let's look at how you should open the conversation with your Architecture AI.

Example Prompt:

Act as a Senior Systems Architect and CTO. I am the solo founder. We are going to design the technical architecture for my new application. Before I share the Core Blueprint, you must agree to the following constraints for our design:

1. Simplicity: Reject over-engineering. Favor understandable solutions.

2. Security & Privacy: Minimal data collection, secure by default.

3. Scalability: Decoupled APIs/functions that can handle growth.

4. Low-Cost: Serverless, generous free-tier tools, lean infrastructure.

5. AI-Friendly: We will only use languages and frameworks that LLMs are highly proficient at writing.

Do you understand these constraints? If so, reply 'ACKNOWLEDGED' and I will provide the Core Blueprint.

Action Steps for the Design Discussion

Open a fresh, dedicated AI chat session. Name it 'Architecture Team'.
Paste the Constraints Prompt to establish the rules of engagement.
Wait for the AI to acknowledge, then paste your Core Blueprint (developed in Chapter number 3).
Ask the AI to propose three different architectural paths: The Leanest, The Most Scalable, and The Recommended Hybrid.

Selecting the Right Stack: Mobile, Web, or SaaS

The 'stack' refers to the combination of technologies used to build your application. The first major fork in the road is determining the delivery mechanism. Will your users access this through a web browser, a mobile app downloaded from an app store, or an API integration?
This decision profoundly impacts your Context Memory Optimization. Building a native mobile app requires managing the complexities of iOS and Android ecosystems, app store reviews, and heavy front-end code. This consumes massive amounts of prompt tokens when asking the AI to debug. A web application, however, is much lighter and easier for an AI to troubleshoot.

Concept: The Delivery Mechanism Matrix

Use this framework to decide your stack based on the business problem:
The Web App (The Default Choice): Choose this 80% of the time. It works on desktops, tablets, and phones via the browser. It bypasses App Store fees. It is incredibly easy for AI to write and deploy. If your app is primarily about viewing data, filling out forms, or managing a dashboard, build a Web App.
The Native Mobile App (The Hardware Choice): Choose this ONLY if your Core Blueprint requires native hardware features that web browsers cannot access cleanly (e.g., heavy background GPS tracking, complex push notifications, offline-first syncing, or augmented reality).

The API / SaaS (The Invisible Choice): Choose this if your product is a service that other businesses will plug into their existing tools (e.g., a data enrichment tool for Salesforce). The 'front-end' is minimal; the value is in the back-end processing.

Example: The SeatSync Stack Decision
Let's return to our running example, SeatSync, the reservation app for remote workers at coffee shops. A novice founder might immediately say, 'I need an iPhone app!' But let's look at it through the lens of Simplicity and Low-Cost.
A native iOS app means dealing with Apple's 30% cut, long review times, and writing Swift code (which AI is good at, but not as good as web languages). Instead, the founder asks the Architecture AI to evaluate the stack.

Example Prompt: *Architecture AI, based on the SeatSync Core Blueprint (booking seats at coffee shops, viewing availability, simple payments), evaluate whether we should build a Native iOS/Android app or a Progressive Web App (PWA). Optimize for my constraints: Low-cost, fast time-to-market, and AI-friendly maintenance.*

The AI correctly advises a Progressive Web App (PWA). A PWA looks and feels like a mobile app on a phone, but it is built using standard web technologies. It is entirely serverless, bypasses the App Store, and is significantly cheaper to host. On most mobile phones you can save a URL using the option 'Add to home screen', which makes your Web App appear like a mobile app. By choosing a web app, the founder just saved hundreds of hours of debugging and optimized their token usage for the rest of the project.

Choosing Your Languages: Prioritizing AI Proficiency
In the traditional development world, you choose a language based on team expertise or specific performance benchmarks. In the age of the AI coding, you choose a language based on the volume of training data the AI has consumed.
Large Language Models are trained on public repositories like GitHub. Therefore, the AI is a world-class expert in the most

popular languages, and merely 'adequate' at niche languages. If you choose a niche language, the AI will hallucinate more often, struggle to find bugs, and waste your context window.

Concept: The Tier 1 AI Languages

To ensure Simplicity and Context Memory Optimization, you must build your stack using Tier 1 AI languages:

Front-End: JavaScript or TypeScript. Frameworks like React, Next.js, or simple Vanilla JS with HTML/CSS. The AI has seen billions of lines of React code. It rarely makes structural mistakes here.

Back-End: Python or Node.js (JavaScript). Python is arguably the absolute best language for AI generation. It is highly readable, which aligns with our Simplicity philosophy. It is also the native language of AI integrations, making it future-proof. For our sample Web App 'SeatSync' we will take you to another level of simplicity where we will let our web frontend TypeScript functions make calls to the backend database on Supabase and for financial transactions or anything needing extra secure handling we will use a feature of Supabase called Edge function. This will be our backend. This will simplify our architecture from hosting a backend running Python API.

Action Steps for Language Selection

Standardize on TypeScript/React for everything the user sees. If you want the ultimate simple stack, use Node.js on the back-end so both your front-end and back-end functions are written in the same language (JavaScript/TypeScript).

The Database Dilemma: Relational vs. NoSQL

The database is the beating heart of your application. If you design the database poorly, scaling becomes a nightmare, and your privacy guarantees crumble. There are generally two paths: Relational (SQL) and NoSQL (Document).

Concept: The Shape of Your Data

Relational databases (like PostgreSQL or MySQL) store data in strict, interconnected tables. They are perfect for highly

structured data where relationships matter (e.g., A User has many Orders; an Order has many Items).
NoSQL databases (like Firebase Firestore or MongoDB) store data in flexible JSON-like documents. They are incredibly fast to set up and scale effortlessly, but can become messy if your data relationships are highly complex.

Fig 4-1

For the solo founder using AI, Serverless NoSQL (like Firebase) or Serverless Postgres (like Supabase) align perfectly with our Low-Cost and Scalability philosophies.

Example: Structuring SeatSync's Database

Let's look at how the founder uses the Architecture AI to define the database for SeatSync. They feed the AI the Data Logic Contract.

Example Prompt: *Architecture AI, we are building SeatSync. I need to choose between a serverless PostgreSQL database (Supabase) and a NoSQL database (Firebase). The core data models are: Users, CoffeeShops, and Reservations. A User can have multiple Reservations. A Coffee Shop has many Reservations. We need to prevent double-booking a seat. Analyze this based on our 'Simplicity' and 'Security' constraints and recommend the database.*

The AI analyzes the request. Because preventing double-booking requires strict transactional integrity (ensuring two people don't book the exact same seat at the exact same millisecond), the AI recommends PostgreSQL.

The SeatSync Architecture Session: Putting It Together
Let us review the complete architectural output for SeatSync after the founder completed their discussion with the Virtual CTO(AI Architecture Chat). This is the exact blueprint that will be handed to the Front-End virtual teams in the next chapters.
Application Type: Progressive Web App (PWA) optimized for mobile screens.
Front-End Stack: React (Next.js) with Tailwind CSS. (Why? AI writes Tailwind CSS perfectly, ensuring fast, beautiful UI without custom CSS files).
Back-End Stack: For our example application we will use Supabase Edge Functions. Our example application SeatSync the frontend will directly call the Supabase Edge Function simplifying the architecture further.
Database: Serverless PostgreSQL via Supabase. (Why? Strict relational data for reservations, built-in security, generous free tier).
Hosting: Vercel for Front-end, Supabase for Back-end/DB. (Why? Zero dev-ops. Push code and it goes live automatically).

Security, Privacy, and Scale by Default
Notice how our philosophies naturally emerged from these choices. By choosing Vercel and Supabase, we achieved Low-Cost infrastructure with automatic scaling. By choosing PostgreSQL, we established a strong foundation for Security and Data Privacy through row-level security policies.
Most importantly, we optimized for the AI's Context Memory by splitting up in separate teams. Because we chose React most prevalent languages in the AI's training data—we can give the AI shorter prompts and receive highly accurate, bug-free code.

Summary and Next Steps

You are no longer a coder guessing at which technology to use. You are a Systems Architect directing a Virtual CTO. You have established constraints, evaluated the delivery mechanism, selected AI-friendly languages, and chosen a robust database.

Your Action Steps Before Chapter 5:

1. Initiate your Architecture Virtual Team chat using the Constraints Prompt.
2. Present your Core Blueprint and have the AI recommend Web vs. Mobile.
3. Confirm your language choices (prioritizing JS/TS and Python).
4. Finalize your database decision based on the complexity of your data relationships.
5. In chapter 3 we generated the Data logic contract, save the final architectural summary. This becomes your 'Architecture Contract' for the rest of the build.

In the next section we will learn about Taming the Machine – Overcoming AI Limitations a critical skill before we start generating code. In chapter 10 we will take this Architecture Contract and hand it to our Back-End Virtual Team. It is time to start building the components of your application.

Part III: Taming the Machine – Overcoming AI Limitations

Chapter 5: The Context Economy: Mastering Tokens and Memory

I want to tell you a story about a founder named Jim. He had a fantastic idea for a logistics platform, successfully drafted his architectural blueprint. For three weeks, he worked in a single chat window with his AI co-pilot. They wrote database schemas, built user interfaces, and configured servers. It felt like AI will be a great revolution for coding.
But around week four, the magic turned into a nightmare. The AI suddenly started suggesting code for a MongoDB database, even though they had spent a week setting up PostgreSQL. It forgot the name of his main CSS file. When he asked it to fix a simple button, it hallucinated an entirely new, broken architecture. Frustrated, Jim concluded that AI just wasn't 'ready' yet to build complex software.
Jim didn't fail because the AI lacked intelligence. He failed because he went bankrupt in the Context Economy.

I can tell you a secret: AI does not have a memory. Not in the human sense. To succeed as a Solo Founder, you must fundamentally change how you view your conversations with Generative AI. You are not talking to a colleague who remembers what you said yesterday. Whether you are polite to it or curt does not matter. You are dealing with a brilliant amnesiac machine who must reread your entire project history every single time you press 'send.'

In this chapter, we will master the ***Context Economy***. You will learn what ***tokens*** are, how the context window actually works, and why ***hallucinations*** happen. Most importantly, I will give you the tools to create 'Core Design Artifacts'—shared

knowledge documents that keep your project running efficiently, cleanly, and at a radically low cost.
These are the critical knowledge for AI coding, we will cover this topic in two subsequent chapters.

The Anatomy of AI Memory: Tokens and Context Windows

Before we can optimize, we must understand the machinery. Let's define the two most important terms in Generative AI: Tokens and the Context Window.

Concept: What is a Token?

When you type a sentence into an AI, it does not read words; it reads 'tokens.' A token is a chunk of text. In English, a token is typically about four characters, or roughly three-quarters of a word. A short word like 'cat' is one token. A longer word like 'architecture' might be broken into three tokens: 'arch', 'itec', 'ture'.
Why does this matter? Because every AI model has a strict, mathematical limit on how many tokens it can process at one time.

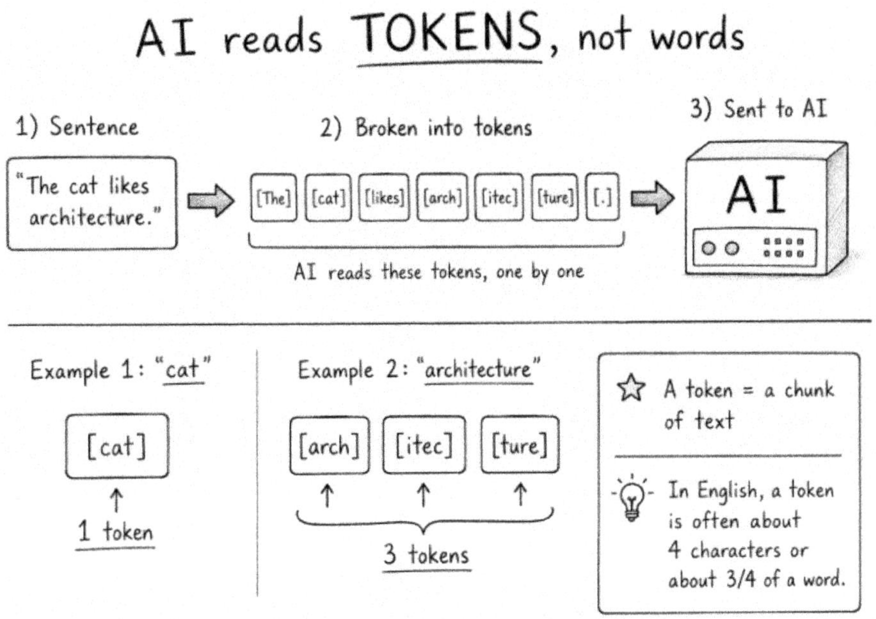

Fig 5-1

This tokenization is essential for the LLM's underlying statistical engine to successfully predict the next word for your answer. This is also the reason why a LLM does not understand what you are saying in a 'human' way.

Concept: The Context Window (The AI's Brain Space)

The Context Window is the absolute maximum number of tokens the AI can hold in its 'working memory' during a single turn of conversation. Think of the context window as a bucket. If a model has a 128,000-token context window, that bucket can hold about a 300-page book.

Here is the critical knowledge that most people miss: Large Language Models (LLMs) are completely stateless. When you chat with an AI, the chat interface gives the illusion of a continuous conversation. Behind the scenes, that is a lie.

Every single time you ask a new question, the application takes your prompt, attaches it to the entire history of the conversation, and sends the whole massive bundle back to the AI. The AI reads the entire transcript from 'Hello' to your current question, generates the next few words, and then forgets everything again.

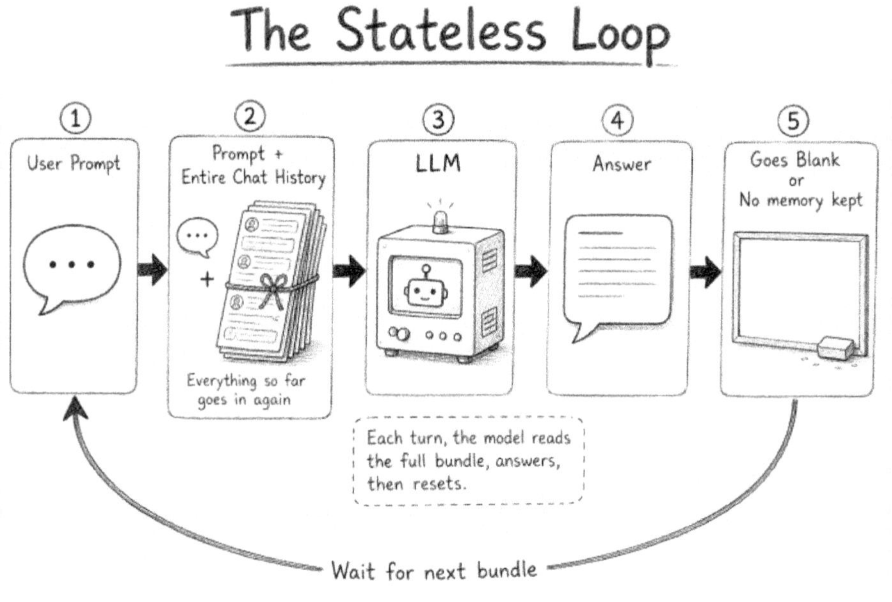

Fig 5-2

If your chat history is 100,000 tokens long, you are forcing the AI to read a 250-page book every time you ask it to fix a typo. This is computationally expensive, slow, and worst of all, it leads to the dreaded 'Hallucination Horizon.' AI platforms struggle with long chats.

The Hallucination Horizon: Why AI Loses its Mind

When you stuff too much information into the context window, the AI begins to hallucinate—making up facts, libraries, or code that do not exist. Let me explain the mechanics of why this happens: Attention Dilution.

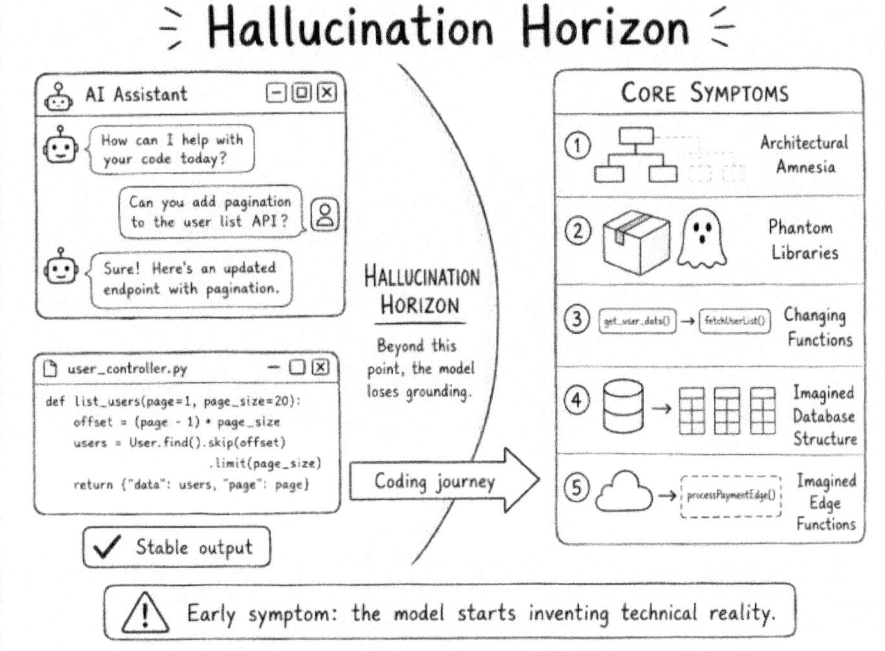

Fig 5-3

Concept: The 'Lost in the Middle' Phenomenon
Modern LLMs use a mechanism called 'Attention.' They look at every token in the context window and calculate how strongly it relates to every other token. Research into LLM architecture reveals a phenomenon known as the 'Lost in the Middle' effect. This is discussed in detail in research paper ***"Lost in the Middle: How Language Models Use Long Contexts" by Nelson F. Liu, Kevin Lin, John Hewitt, Ashwin Paranjape, Michele Bevilacqua, Fabio Petroni, and Percy Liang***.

LLMs are highly proficient at remembering information at the very beginning of a prompt (your system instructions) and information at the very end (your most recent message). But the massive middle chunk of the conversation? The AI's attention gets diluted. It may gloss over it. The model learns statistically that most of the answers to your prompts are towards the beginning(primacy bias) and end of the conversation (recency bias) and a sharp performance drop happens when the answer is in the middle part of the conversation. This develops naturally from the statistical engine underlying the architecture of LLMs. The latest LLM versions have introduced various techniques like architectural, training, and retrieval-aware innovations that ***reduce*** mid-context failure mode. Claude and Gemini are doing better in this battle. At the time of writing this book this issue still remained as the most serious challenge to coding projects.

When the AI encounters a gap in its attention, it relies on its probabilistic training data to fill the void. If it forgets that you are using PostgreSQL, it might default to MongoDB simply because MongoDB is statistically very popular in its training data for web apps.

Example: The SeatSync Token Bloat

Imagine you are building SeatSync, our coffee shop reservation app. You have a single chat window titled 'App Build.'

Week 1: You paste in your Blueprint. (2,000 tokens).

Week 2: You paste in the backend code to debug a login issue. (10,000 tokens).

Week 3: You have long debates about button colors, paste in five different React components, and fix a dozen typos. (50,000 tokens).

Week 4: You ask, 'Write the function to create a new reservation.'

Because your context window is bloated with irrelevant arguments about button colors, the AI's attention is diluted. It misses the database rules you established in Week 2. It hallucinates a reservation function that doesn't check for double-booking, potentially destroying your app's core value proposition.

Action Steps: Recognizing the Hallucination Horizon

You have reached the *Hallucination Horizon* when you see these symptoms:

The ***AI apologizes but repeats the same coding error***.

It suggests using a ***library or language that you explicitly decided against earlier***.

Responses take ***significantly longer*** to generate.
The code it ***outputs is completely disjointed from the surrounding files***.
When this happens, you cannot 'fix' it by arguing with the AI. Arguing just adds more tokens to the bucket. You must abandon the chat and use the *Isolated Context Methodologies* expanded in the next chapter.

Core Design Artifacts: The Anchor of Your Virtual Teams
To avoid the Hallucination Horizon, ***we never use one mega-chat window***. As discussed in Chapter 3, we use specialized Virtual Teams (Architecture, Back-End, Front-End). But how do we keep these separate chats perfectly synchronized without bloat?
The answer is *Core Design Artifacts*. These are highly compressed, densely written text files that serve as the single source of truth for your project. You will paste these artifacts into the very first prompt of every new chat window you open.

Concept: The Four Essential Artifacts
Instead of relying on chat history, we rely on state documents. You only need four:
1. ***The Core Blueprint:*** The business logic. Who is the user, what is the problem, and what are the constraints?
2. ***The Data Logic Contract:*** The exact database schema. The names of the tables, the columns, and the relationships.
3. ***The Interface Contract:*** The API endpoints. How the front-end asks the back-end for data.
4. ***State Summary Document:*** The State Summary Document is a **highly compressed** summary of the current reality of that specific virtual team. It bridges the gap between the static Core Blueprint and the current state of your code.
By feeding these four documents to a fresh AI chat, you are instantly downloading the entire 'state' of your project into the AI's brain with zero bloat. The AI knows exactly what to do, and 100% of its attention is focused on the immediate task.

Example: Generating the State Summary Document for SeatSync

Before leaving the exhausted Frontend Virtual Team chat, you ask the AI to summarize its work. You do not want every line of code; you want the architecture of the code.
PROMPT TO GENERATE STATE SUMMARY DOCUMENT:

This chat is getting too long, and we need to migrate to a new window. Please generate a dense 'State Summary Document' for the Frontend Virtual Team.

Include:
1. A file tree of the React components we have built so far.
2. The exact Tailwind global configurations we finalized.
3. The names of the 3 custom hooks we created for state management.
4. The current bug we were trying to fix (the Cancel Reservation routing issue).

Output only Markdown. Be concise. Do not output actual component code.

The AI gives you a crisp, 200-word + Markdown summary. This is your State Summary Document

Example: Drafting the Data Logic Contract for SeatSync
Let's look at how *dense* and specific a Core Design Artifact should be. Notice the lack of conversational fluff.
BAD example (Too conversational, wastes tokens):
'Hey, so we decided that for SeatSync we are going to use a Postgres database. We need a table for users, and they should have an email and a password. Also we need coffee shops, and they need a name and location. Users can book seats, so make a reservation table too.'

GOOD example (Dense, explicit, token-efficient):
'DATA LOGIC CONTRACT - SEATSYNC (PostgreSQL)
TABLE: Users (id UUID PK, email VARCHAR UNIQUE, created_at TIMESTAMP)
TABLE: Shops (id UUID PK, name VARCHAR, capacity INT)
TABLE: Reservations (id UUID PK, user_id UUID FK, shop_id

UUID FK, start_time TIMESTAMP, end_time TIMESTAMP) CONSTRAINT: Prevent overlapping start_time/end_time for the same shop_id.'

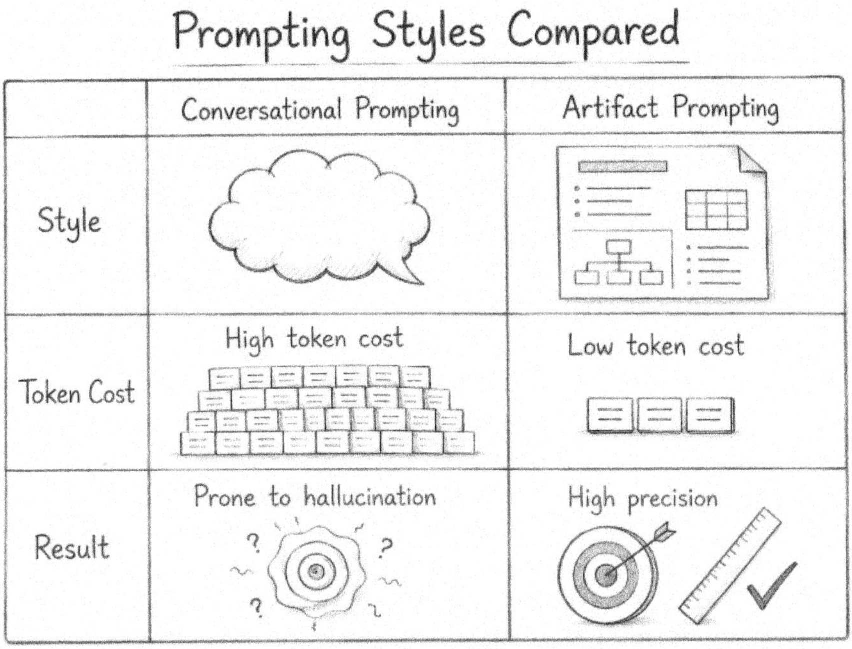

Fig 5-4

Action Steps: Creating Your Artifacts

Never write these artifacts yourself. Use the Architecture chat from Chapter 4 to generate them.
Prompt the AI: '*Summarize our database schema into a highly compressed Data Logic Contract. Remove all conversational filler. Use strict technical notation. Keep it under 500 words.*'
Save these artifacts in a dedicated folder on your computer (e.g., a Notion page or a simple text file directory).

Whenever you update your app's logic, update the artifact file immediately. The artifact is your projects 'application architect'; the chat window is just a temporary workspace. Create these artifacts time to time for each of your AI Virtual teams and version and save them on your computer folder.

Best Practices for Token Optimization (The Context Economy)

Now that we have our artifacts, we must practice strict token budgeting in our daily workflow. The more tokens you save, the faster the AI replies, the less it hallucinates, and the cheaper your API bills will be if you are using paid developer platforms.

Concept: Semantic Compression

As an AI prompt engineer, one of the most powerful techniques I use is called *Semantic Compression*. LLMs are incredibly good at unpacking dense jargon. You do not need to speak to them in polite, complete English sentences. This represents a profound shift from the traditional software engineering paradigm, where ensuring source code was easily readable by other human developers stood as a non-negotiable requirement.

You can compress complex ideas into shorthand, and the AI will expand it perfectly. For example, instead of explaining exactly how you want a modern, clean, mobile-first user interface with shadows and rounded corners, you can just say: *'UI: TailwindCSS, mobile-first, clean modern SaaS aesthetic, deep shadows.'*

That saves hundreds of tokens and yields the exact same result. It is highly precise and *information heavy 'AI speak'.*

Concept: Surgical Code Pasting

The number one way founders waste tokens is by pasting an entire 1,000-line code file into the chat just to ask why one button isn't working.

Instead, practice Surgical Code Pasting. If the error is in the 'Submit Reservation' function, only paste that function, along with the relevant imports. The AI does not need to see your navigation bar code to fix a database query.
If you have to upload a full program specifically tell your AI prompt to provide you the 'surgically change' to the code needed. ***Avoid asking the AI to regenerate the full code file again as much as you can.*** This would risk the AI replacing a perfectly working part of the code in the file, which you did not ask for. If you do ask for a full file rewrite then compare the old file with the new code file to make sure important comment lines or code lines have not been lost or 'optimized'. In the new world this should trigger a code review. I have developed special tools to do this. I never accept a fully regenerated code file without this automated review identifying all changes. You too can generate your own tool see appendix E.

Example: The 'Shrink Ray' Prompt
If you find yourself in a chat window that has successfully solved a tough problem, but the chat is now horribly long, use the *'Shrink Ray'* prompt and generate a '***State Summary Document'*** before abandoning the chat.

'We have successfully built the authentication module. Before we close this session, I need you to compress your knowledge. Write a highly technical, dense summary of the exact authentication flow, libraries used, and environment variables required. Output this as a single paragraph with zero conversational filler. I will use this to prime our next chat.'
The AI will output an incredibly dense paragraph. You copy that paragraph save it on your local pc. Then open a brand new chat, paste it in, and continue working flawlessly with a completely refreshed context window.

Summary and Next Steps
You are no longer treating the AI like a human colleague. You recognize it as a powerful, stateless, probabilistic generation

engine. By understanding the boundaries of the Context Window, you can prevent the *Hallucination Horizon*. By utilizing *Core Design Artifacts*, you anchor every Virtual Team to a single source of truth.

Your Action Steps Before Chapter 6:

1. Go back to your Architecture chat from Chapter 4.
2. Ask the AI to draft your three Core Design Artifacts: The Core Blueprint, The Data Logic Contract, and The Interface Contract.
3. Generate State Summary Document' for all sessions you have up to now.
4. Save these documents locally. They are the keys to your kingdom.
5. Practice Semantic Compression. See how few words you can use to communicate a complex idea to the AI. We will call this '***AI speak***'.

In chapter 6 we will learn how to diagnose and treat hallucination when it is still manageable. With our artifacts in hand and our token budget optimized, we are ready to write code.

Chapter 6: Diagnosing and Treating Hallucinations

You have spent the first five chapters of this book acting as the ultimate Systems Architect for the new world of AI coding. You mapped out your vision in Part I, built a robust, scalable blueprint using the Context Economy in Part II. You are moving fast. You are building SeatSync, our coffee shop reservation app, with a fraction of the time and capital it historically takes, you are saving tens of thousands of dollars. In the last chapter you were introduced to the concepts of tokens, context memory and hallucination, hallucination horizon. In this chapter we will dive deeper to find ways to minimize the negative sides of those challenges.
We will cover how to establish strict checkpoints to preserve your code's integrity, and, most importantly, the exact tactical prompt engineering techniques you can use to overcome this challenge.

Concept: The Three Types of Code Hallucinations
When you are functioning as a solo founder using AI as your engineering department, you will typically encounter three specific types of hallucinations:
1. ***Architectural Amnesia:*** The AI forgets the foundational decisions you made earlier in the conversation. It might switch from your chosen PostgreSQL database back to MongoDB, or forget that SeatSync is a Progressive Web App (PWA) and start trying to write React Native code.
2. ***Phantom Libraries:*** The AI invents a software package or a library that perfectly solves your problem, but does not exist in reality. It wants to be helpful, so it hallucinated an elegant, one-line solution that will fail the moment you try to compile your code.
3. ***Documentation Injection:*** The AI accurately remembers the library you are using (e.g., Supabase), but it hallucinates the specific methods or API endpoints, usually by confusing it with

an older version of the library or mixing it with a competitor's API (like Firebase).

Example: The SeatSync Phantom Library

Imagine you are building the real-time seat availability feature for SeatSync. You are using React for the frontend and Supabase for the backend. You ask the AI to write a hook that listens for database changes when a seat is reserved.
The AI responds with this brilliantly simple, clean code:

```
import { useRealtimeSubscription } from '@supabase/react-
hooks';

const useSeatStatus = (shopId) => {
  const { data } = useRealtimeSubscription('seats',{ shop_id:
shopId });
  return data;
};
```

It looks beautiful. It looks exactly like how modern React code should look. The problem? As of this writing, there is no official `@supabase/react-hooks` library containing a `useRealtimeSubscription` method. The AI synthesized the concepts of 'React hooks' and 'Supabase real-time subscriptions' and hallucinated a phantom library.

Action Steps: Early Detection

How do you catch this before it breaks your build? You must cultivate a healthy skepticism.

- Step 1: ***Verify the Imports***. Every time the AI introduces a new import statement or a new library in your code, stop. Do a quick web search or check the official documentation. Do not assume the library exists just because the code is formatted beautifully.
- Step 2: ***Watch for Tone Shifts***. Often, when an LLM is hallucinating, *its output becomes more generalized.* If it stops referencing your specific Core Design Artifacts (the Blueprint, Data Logic Contract, Interface Contract) and starts writing generic tutorial-style code, it is losing context.

• Step 3: ***Run the Code Often***. If you are generating multiple codes or updating multiple code files the longer you go without running/testing the new generated code risk of code failure increases. The fastest way to catch a phantom library or a documentation injection is a compiler error. Delaying execution/testing allows hallucinations to compound.

Example: Diagnosing Context Saturation

Let's say you've been working on the SeatSync dashboard for 5 days in the same chat window. You ask it to add a filter for 'available power outlets.' The AI provides the code, but it uses a completely different CSS naming convention than the Tailwind CSS you've been using last 2 days.

You have hit the ***Hallucination Horizon***. The AI hasn't gone rogue; it has simply dropped the middle context where you established Tailwind as the standard.

Action Steps: Token Monitoring via Diagnostic Prompts

You cannot natively 'see' a token counter in most standard AI chat interfaces(some AI platforms do show this), but you can use your prompt engineering skills to diagnose the machine's memory health. You do this by injecting ***'Diagnostic Prompts***.' When you suspect the AI is losing the plot, pause your coding requests and send a prompt explicitly designed to test its current context memory. Ask it specially crafted questions:

DIAGNOSTIC PROMPT:

Before we write the next component, I need to check our alignment.

1. Summarize the exact tech stack we are using for the frontend and backend in bullet points.

2. State the last strict constraint I gave you regarding database access.

3. Based on our conversation so far, what is the name of our core design artifact controlling the UI?

If the AI answers these accurately, your context is still healthy. If it hallucinates the answers—saying you are using Firebase instead of Supabase, or forgetting the Interface Contract—you have definitively crossed the Hallucination Horizon. It is time to remedy the decay.

Reference: Towards Long Context Hallucination Detection. *arXiv.* https://doi.org/10.48550/arxiv.2504.19457

Concept: Distinguishing Conversation Lengths
Understanding when to transplant the brain relies on recognizing where your Virtual Team sits in its lifecycle:

1. ***The Short Conversation*** (0-8K tokens): Highly agile. Maximum reasoning capacity. Perfect recall of instructions. This is where you want to be when tackling complex logic or core architectural decisions.
2. ***The Medium Conversation*** (8K-32K tokens): The working state. The AI still functions well but may suffer from the 'Lost in the Middle' effect. It might forget minor styling preferences or a rule established in prompt 5. Responses take longer to generate as the context window fills.
3. ***The Long Conversation*** (32K+ tokens): The danger zone. Sluggish generation, frequent hallucinations, and Architectural Amnesia. The AI begins apologizing frequently and overwriting perfectly good code. A '*Brain Transplant*' is mandatory.

Note 5: *Assume 1 word = 1.2 -1.4 tokens in your chat. I am including the input and output tokens. Based on your model the above ranges will differ. Newer frontier models will have much higher thresholds than in above example, but they are not free from hallucination. See* ***Appendix B*** *for monitoring token usage locally on your windows system.*

Example: The SeatSync UI Virtual Team's Exhaustion
Imagine you are running the 'Frontend Virtual Team' for SeatSync. You've spent 35 prompts developing the React components, tweaking Tailwind classes, and setting up routing. The chat is now taking 20 seconds just to start typing a response. You ask it to add a simple 'Cancel Reservation'

button, and it suddenly hallucinates a totally different routing library. You have hit the ***Very Long Conversation*** stage.

Establishing Strict Checkpoints

The best remedy for hallucinations is prevention. In software engineering, we use version control systems like Git to save our progress. When working with AI, you must adopt ***Checkpoint Driven Development*** (CDD).

Concept: The Checkpoint Protocol

A checkpoint is a deliberate pause in generation where you stop, test the code, verify its alignment with your Core Design Artifacts, and save the '*State Summary Document*'. *You never ask the AI to build feature B until feature A is fully checkpointed and tested in your local environment.*

Example: The SeatSync Reservation Flow

You are building the mechanism for a user to book a seat at 'Roasters Coffee.' You do not write one massive prompt: 'Build the reservation frontend, the API endpoint, and the database logic.' That is a guaranteed recipe for hallucinations.

Instead, you establish checkpoints:

Checkpoint 1: Establish the Supabase table and RLS policy. (Test in Supabase dashboard. Save schema to Data Logic Contract).

Checkpoint 2: Write the backend edge function. (Test with Postman or cURL. Save endpoint spec).

Checkpoint 3: Write the Next.js frontend form. (Test in local browser).

Action Steps: Enforcing Checkpoints

• Step 1: Break your feature into isolated components (Database, Backend, Frontend).

• Step 2: Use the 'Boundary Forcing' technique when prompting, explicitly forbid the AI from moving to the next checkpoint.

Example:

'Write the database schema. DO NOT write the edge functions. Stop and wait for my approval.'

• Step 3: Once a checkpoint is verified locally, update your Core Artifacts. These artifacts act as your ground truth, ensuring the AI cannot hallucinate past decisions.

Tactical Cures: Steering Back to Reality

Even with checkpoints and context compression, the AI will occasionally slip up and hallucinate a function or library. When this happens, how you react determines whether you spend five minutes fixing it, or two hours fighting the machine.

Concept: The Ground Truth Anchor

Amateur prompt engineers argue with the AI. They type: 'That library doesn't exist, try again.' This is highly inefficient. The AI might just hallucinate a *second* fake library.

As a professional, you must provide the AI with Ground Truth. You must act as the bridge between the AI's isolated environment and the real world. You do this through a technique called ***Documentation Injection***.

Example: Curing the Supabase Hallucination

Let's return to our earlier example. The AI hallucinated the `useRealtimeSubscription` method. You got a compiler error. Instead of just telling the AI it is wrong, you go to the actual Supabase documentation online. You find the correct way to subscribe to real-time changes using their standard JavaScript client.

Action Steps: The Anchor Prompting Technique

When a hallucination occurs, use the Anchor Prompting framework to correct it instantly:

• Step 1: *Identify the failure* (e.g., 'The code threw an error because useRealtimeSubscription does not exist').

• Step 2: *Fetch the Ground Truth* (COPY A SNIPPET FROM THE OFFICIAL, CURRENT DOCUMENTATION).

• Step 3*: Inject and Steer.* Combine the error and the documentation into a single, decisive prompt.
EXAMPLE ANCHOR PROMPT:
The previous code failed. The library '@SUPABASE/REACT-HOOKS' *does not have that method.*

I have retrieved the current official documentation for Supabase real-time subscriptions. Here is the exact snippet of how it should be done:

[PASTE DOCUMENTATION SNIPPET HERE]

Based ONLY on this documentation snippet, rewrite our SeatSync realtime listener component. Do not use any external hook libraries. Use standard React useEffect and the Supabase client provided in the docs.

By doing this, you override the AI's probabilistic guessing with hard, deterministic facts. You have steered it back to reality.

Conclusion
Hallucinations are not bugs; they are a fundamental architectural characteristic of Generative AI technology. They are the price we pay for a system capable of immense creativity and reasoning. But as a solo founder acting as the Systems Architect, you are not a passive consumer of this technology. You are the pilot.
By maintaining strict ***checkpoints***, actively ***monitoring*** *the context window* through diagnostic prompts, compressing state before the horizon collapses, and aggressively injecting ***ground truth*** when errors occur, you tame the machine. You transform it from unpredictable oracle into a reliable, tireless engineering department.
In the next chapter, we will delve in the concept of the ***'Brain Transplant'***. We will explore advanced Context Transfer Strategies, enabling you to manage massive codebases seamlessly across dozens of isolated virtual teams.

Chapter 7: The "Brain Transplant": Context Transfer Strategies

The massive neural networks process millions of tokens a second. Capabilities of LLMs are awe-inspiring when their context is pristine, and I have witnessed their complete intellectual collapse when their context window overflows. As 'Solo Founder' one of your core task now is to manage context of your AI chats.

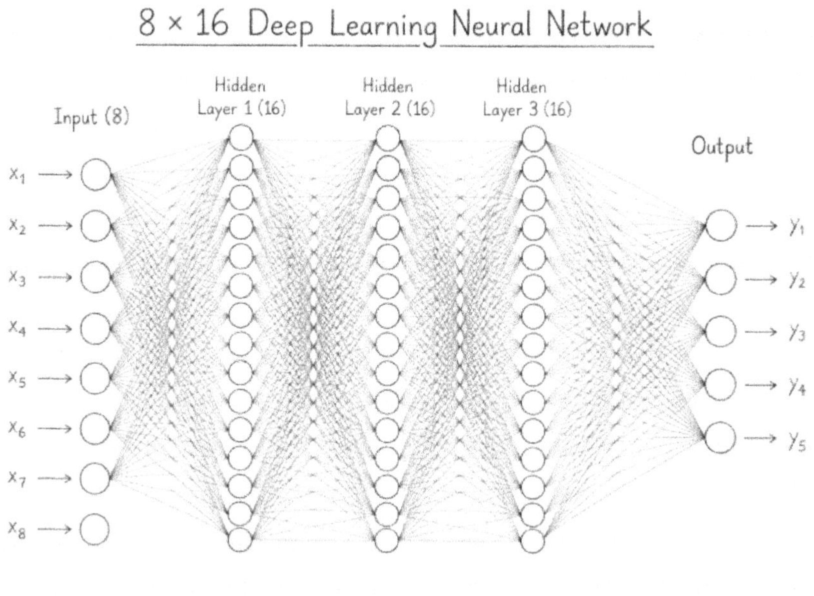

Fig 7-1 A simple representation of neural network your prompt passes through.

In Chapter 3, we established a foundational paradigm shift: ***A Team is a Chat Tab***. You isolated your development into Virtual Teams to respect the AI's active memory limit. By doing that we broke down the context window into manageable chunks significantly reducing hallucinations and managed to preserve your project knowledge.

In Chapter 5, we discussed how to detect the Hallucination Horizon—the moment the AI starts making things up because it has forgotten the middle of your conversation. In Chapter 6 we delved into diagnosing and treating Hallucinations.
But what happens when a Virtual Team is fundamentally exhausted? When a chat becomes too long, sluggish, or repeatedly forgets its instructions? You cannot simply keep typing. You cannot force an overloaded neural network to 'remember better.' You must execute a '***Brain Transplant***'.

A Brain Transplant is the strategic extraction of a project's current state from an exhausted chat window, and the seamless transfer of that knowledge into a brand-new, highly responsive chat window. In this chapter, we will master this technique.
We will cover how to prepare for it from Day Zero, the precise artifacts required, how to update your *Core Blueprint* without causing context bloat, use *State Summary Document* and even how to recover if the transplant fails.

Day Zero Readiness: Designing for the Transplant
You do not prepare for a Brain Transplant when the chat is failing. You prepare for it on Day Zero. A successful transplant requires structured artifacts that can easily be picked up by a fresh AI chat (a new virtual team)

Concept: State Summary Document
In Chapter 3, we introduced 'Document 1: The Core Blueprint'. This is your single source of truth, pasted into the very first prompt of every new Virtual Team. It aligns all teams on the project's key goals.
But when you perform a Brain Transplant for a specific Virtual Team, you need more than just the Blueprint. You need the '*State Summary Document*'—the precise work that this specific team has accomplished since the chat began. See chapter 5 for example prompt to generate it.

Action Steps: Executing the Brain Transplant

Step 1: Generate the **State Summary Document** in the dying chat window.
Step 2: Open a brand-new, empty chat tab. This is your new Virtual Team environment.
Step 3: Paste Document 1 (The Core Blueprint) to establish the baseline soul of the project.
Step 4: Paste the **State Summary Document** immediately below it.
Step 5: Command the fresh AI to acknowledge the context and resume work on the current bug.

INITIALIZATION PROMPT FOR NEW CHAT:
You are the new Frontend Virtual Team for SeatSync.

[PASTE CORE BLUEPRINT]

[PASTE STATE SUMMARY DOCUMENT]

Read the above carefully to synchronize your memory. Reply 'ACKNOWLEDGED' and provide a plan to fix the 'Cancel Reservation routing issue' mentioned in the State Summary Document.

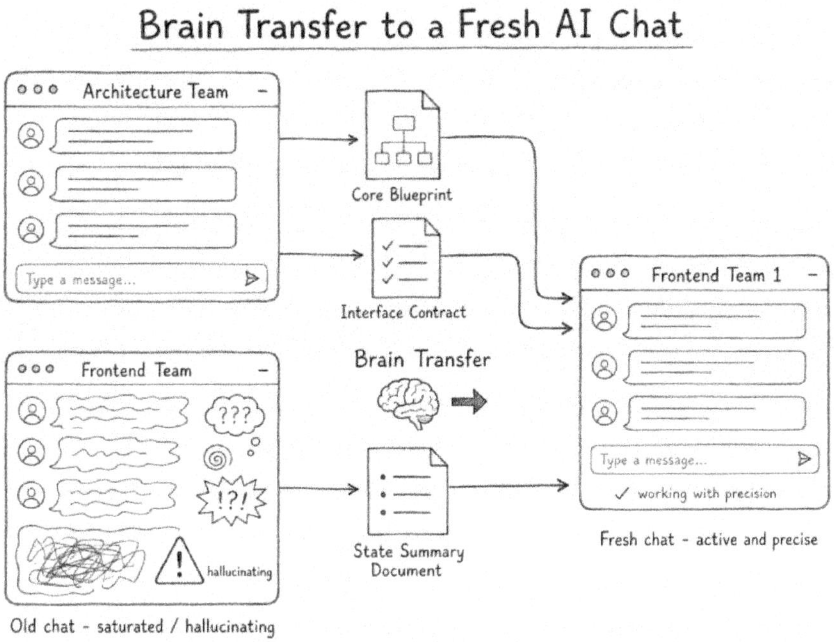

Fig 7-2

Updating the Core Blueprint: Managing the Ripple Effect
The effect of downstream document changes on upstream documents. A critical question arises during this process: If the Frontend Team made significant discoveries, should I update the Core Blueprint so that ALL Virtual Teams know about it? As AI engineer knowing LLMs, my answer is a strict: *No, unless absolutely necessary*. Context memory is expensive and fragile. If you bloat the Core Blueprint with frontend-specific details, you will degrade the reasoning capacity of your Backend Virtual Team.

Concept: The Interface Contract Rule

How do you decide what makes it into the Core Blueprint? You use the Interface Contract Rule. *You only update the Core Blueprint if a decision made by one Virtual Team fundamentally changes how another Virtual Team must interact with it.*

Example: Good vs. Bad Blueprint Updates
Scenario A: Your Frontend Team decides to switch a button color from blue to indigo.
Does this affect the backend? No.
Do you update the Core Blueprint? No. That detail stays in the Frontend State Summary Document.
Scenario B: Your Frontend Team realizes that SeatSync needs to filter coffee shops by 'Available Outlets'. This requires a new database column.
Does this affect the backend? Yes. It changes the Interface Contract.
Do you update the Core Blueprint? Yes.

Action Steps: The Partial Update Strategy
When a change mandates a Blueprint update, do not rewrite the whole document. Use a 'Partial Update' strategy.
Step 1: Identify the exact line or section in the Core Blueprint that needs modification (e.g., 'Data Models: Added boolean has_outlets to CoffeeShop table').
Step 2: Update your master ***Core Blueprint*** file locally on your computer.
Step 3: Do you need to update the other running Virtual Teams immediately? ***Only if their current task relies on that new data***. If the Backend Team is currently writing user authentication logic, leave them alone. Interrupting them with an irrelevant schema update will only push them closer to their own Hallucination Horizon. Update them on their next natural Brain Transplant.

The Failed Transplant: Recovery and Autopsy

Even with perfect preparation, a Brain Transplant can fail. '*State Summary Document*' might have omitted a crucial, unstated assumption from the previous chat.

Concept: Hallucination Inheritance vs. Loss of Nuance
There are two main reasons a transplant fails:

1. ***Hallucination Inheritance***: The dying chat was already hallucinating when you asked it to generate the State Summary document. It sneaked a fake library or an incorrect database schema into the summary. You blindly pasted it into the new chat, infecting the fresh brain with the old disease.
2. ***Loss of Nuance***: The dying chat summarized perfectly, but left out the 'why'. It noted that you are using a specific custom hook, but forgot to explain the complex edge case that hook solves. The new chat immediately rewrites the hook, breaking the edge case.

Example: Recovering from a Nuance Loss
You start a new Backend chat for SeatSync. You give it the *Blueprint and the* ***State Summary Document***. You ask it to add a new endpoint. The AI writes the endpoint but removes the custom rate-limiting logic you spent two hours perfecting yesterday. The nuance was lost in the transfer.

Action Steps: The Re-Anchor Protocol
Do not panic, and do not spend hours arguing with the new chat. Execute the ***Re-Anchor Protocol:***
Step 1: Stop the current chat. Do not let it continue generating bad code.
Step 2: Go back to the original source code on your local machine. Find the exact block of code that the AI is failing to understand (e.g., the rate-limiting middleware).
Step 3: Use an ***Anchor Prompt*** in the new chat to forcefully inject the missing nuance.

ANCHOR PROMPT:
Stop. You missed a critical piece of context regarding our rate-limiting architecture.
Here is the exact code for our current rate-limiter:
[PASTE CODE]

Analyze this code. Acknowledge why we built it this way, and rewrite your previous response to ensure it integrates seamlessly with this existing logic.

By doing this, you instantly patch the missing hole in the transplanted brain. You have bypassed the flawed summary by providing ground truth from your actual codebase.

Conclusion

Mastering the Brain Transplant is the difference between a frustrated amateur and a highly effective Advanced Prompt Engineer. You cannot out-prompt a saturated Context Window. You must respect the machine's architectural limits. By isolating your teams, monitoring conversation health, diligently maintaining your **Core Blueprint** without bloating it, and mastering the ***State Summary Document***, you ensure your project never loses momentum. Your development cycle becomes an infinite relay race, with fresh, highly capable Virtual Teams passing the baton seamlessly to the next.

If you have reached this milestone in your journey, you now possess the core conceptual framework of an ***Advanced Prompt Engineer***. Congratulations!

In the next section, we set up our local environment and move into coding and serious testing. We will then cover Integration and Quality Assurance—how to make these isolated Virtual Teams talk to each other, and how to use AI to write the tests that ensure your product is bulletproof before launch.

Part IV: The Build – Prompt Engineering for Production

Chapter 8: Setting Up Your Workspace Locally

Welcome to Part IV.
In this chapter, we are going to set up your local development environment from scratch. By the end of this chapter, you will have a structured folder system, version control to track your progress, cloud storage for your code, a powerful text editor, the necessary programming languages installed, and a working local web server.
Do not worry if you have never written a line of code or if terms like "repository" or "local server" sound intimidating. We will take you step by step.

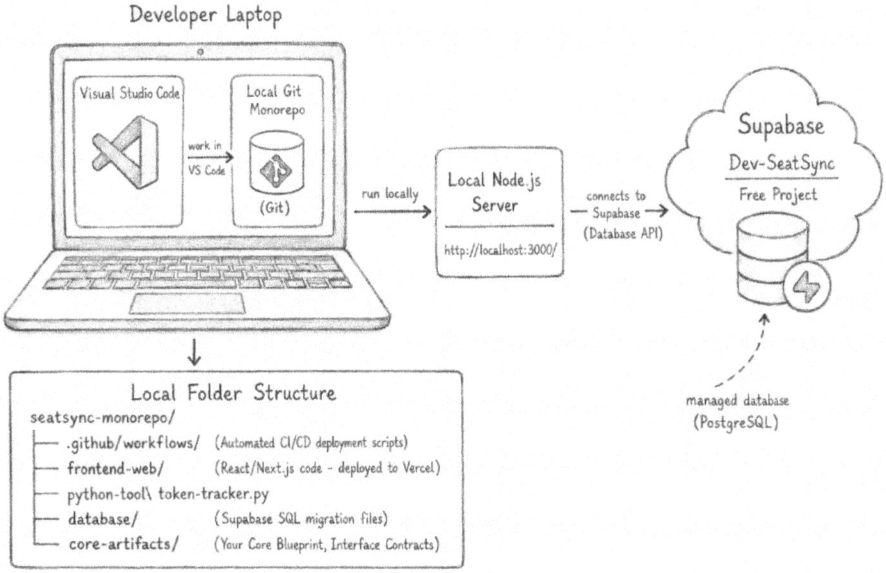

Fig 8-1

1. Creating Your Project Blueprint (Folder Structure)
Concept
When building a complex application like SeatSync, organization is important. Software projects can quickly grow to contain thousands of individual files. If these files are scattered randomly, the project becomes unmanageable. To prevent this, we use a specific architectural pattern called a "***Monorepo***" (short for monolithic repository).
A monorepo simply means that all the different pieces of your application—the frontend website, the backend server, the database configurations, and the documentation—live inside one single, master folder. This makes it incredibly easy to track changes across your entire project simultaneously.

Example
Imagine you are running a restaurant. You could keep your recipes in the kitchen, your employee schedules in the manager's office, and your financial records at your home. This is disjointed. A monorepo is like having a master binder with dedicated, clearly labeled tabs for Recipes, Schedules, and Finances all in one place.
Action Steps
The following steps are optimized for a Windows laptop. If you are using Mac or Ubuntu we will tell you what to do at the end of this chapter, don't worry. Let's create your master folder structure. We are going to place this directly on your C drive for easy access and to avoid long file path errors that can sometimes occur in Windows.
Step 1: Open your File Explorer on your computer.

Step 2: Navigate to your primary local disk, usually labeled as Windows (C:) or Local Disk (C:).

Step 3: Right-click in an empty space, select "New," and then choose "Folder."

Step 4: Name this new folder exactly: seatsync-monorepo

Step 5: Double-click to open your new seatsync-monorepo folder.

Step 6: Inside this folder, create five sub-folders. Right-click, select New > Folder, and create the following one by one:

.github
frontend-web
python-tools
database
core-artifacts

Note 3: *For the .github folder, Windows might prompt you if you want to create a folder starting with a dot. Simply confirm. Inside that .github folder, create one more folder named workflows. as we will use Supabase Edge Functions. We will Keep this folder structure as a place holder for future expansion.*

Here is what each folder does:

• .github/workflows/: This holds Automated CI/CD deployment scripts. Think of it as instructions for robots that will automatically publish your site when you update the code.

• frontend-web/: This will house your React/Next.js code. This is everything the user sees and clicks on (deployed later to a service called Vercel).

• python-tools/: In our case we will develop a support tool in Python. This tool will be kept in this folder.

• database/: This holds Supabase SQL migration files, which are the blueprints for how your database tables are structured. Edge Function code.

• core-artifacts/: A safe place to store your Core Blueprint, Interface Contracts, and project requirements.

2. Setting up Version Control with Git

Concept

As you write code, you will make mistakes. You might accidentally delete a crucial file, or make a change that breaks everything. If you are just using normal folders, recovering lost work is incredibly difficult. Enter "Git."

Git is a version control system. It acts as an advanced "time machine" for your project. Every time you reach a milestone, you tell Git to take a "snapshot" of your entire folder. If something goes wrong tomorrow, you can simply ask Git to rewind your files back to exactly how they looked today.

Example

Think of writing a novel. Instead of having files named Draft1.docx, Draft2_Final.docx, Draft3_REALLY_FINAL.docx cluttering your desktop, Git allows you to just have one file. It remembers every change you ever made in the background, allowing you to instantly revert to yesterday's work if you decide you do not like today's chapter.

Action Steps

Step 1: Open your web browser and go to git-scm.com.

Step 2: Click the prominent "Download for Windows" button.

Step 3: Once the installer downloads, open it.

Step 4: Click "Next" through the installation screens. The default settings are perfectly optimized for beginners. You do not need to change any of the checkboxes.

Step 5: Click "Install" and wait for the process to finish, then click "Finish." Git is now secretly running in the background of your computer, ready to track your files.

3. Connecting to the Cloud (GitHub)

Concept

While Git tracks changes on your local computer, what happens if you spill coffee on your laptop and it breaks? Your local time machine is destroyed along with your code. To truly secure your project, we use GitHub.

GitHub is a cloud-based hosting service for Git repositories. It is essentially an off-site, highly secure vault for your code. By connecting your local Git tracking to GitHub in the cloud, you ensure that every snapshot you take is backed up safely on the internet. Furthermore, when we deploy our app later, the cloud servers will read our code directly from GitHub.

Example

If Git is the local auto-save feature in a video game, GitHub is the "Cloud Sync." If you lose your PC and had to buy a brand new computer, you can log into GitHub and download your entire project exactly as you left it.

Action Steps

First, let's create the cloud vault:

Step 1: Go to github.com and sign up for a free account if you do not already have one. Use a professional email address.

Step 2: Once logged in, look for the "+" icon in the top right corner and select "New repository".

Step 3: Name the repository seatsync-monorepo. It is best practice to keep the cloud name identical to your local folder name.

Step 4: Select the "Private" option. You do not want the whole world seeing your proprietary business code.

Step 5: Do NOT check any boxes for adding a README or .gitignore right now. Keep it completely empty.

Step 6: Click the green "Create repository" button.

Now, keep that GitHub webpage open. We will connect your local folder to this cloud vault in just a few steps, after we install our primary tool: VS Code.

If you run into issues see our example prompt to generate Git install instructions in Appendix D.

4. Equipping Your Workshop (VS Code)

Concept

To write code, you need a specialized text editor. While you technically could write software in Microsoft Notepad, it would be miserable. A modern Integrated Development Environment (IDE) is a smart, powerful tool designed to make writing code as easy as possible. It color-codes your text, points out typos before you run the code, and gives you a command terminal all in one window.

Visual Studio Code (VS Code) is currently the most popular, robust, and free IDE in the world. It will be your primary home for the duration of this project.

Example

Think of Notepad as a simple, manual handsaw. It cuts wood, but it takes immense effort. VS Code is a top-of-the-line electric table saw with laser guides, safety sensors, and automatic measurements. It is built to help you build faster.

Action Steps

Step 1: Go to code.visualstudio.com.

Step 2: Click the massive "Download for Windows" button.

Step 3: Open the downloaded installer and accept the agreement.

Step 4: Click "Next" until you reach the "Select Additional Tasks" screen. CRITICAL: Make sure to check the boxes that say "Add 'Open with Code' action to Windows Explorer file context menu" and "Add 'Open with Code' action to Windows Explorer directory context menu." This makes opening projects incredibly easy later.

Step 5: Ensure "Add to PATH" is also checked, then click "Next" and "Install".

Step 6: Once installed, open VS Code. You will be greeted by a welcome screen. Feel free to choose a Dark or Light theme that is easy on your eyes.

Now, let's open your project. In VS Code, click File > Open Folder... from the top menu, navigate to your C: drive, select the seatsync-monorepo folder, and click "Select Folder". You will now see your folder structure on the left side of the screen.

Linking the Cloud (Completing Step 3)

Now that we have VS Code open, let's execute the commands to link your local code to GitHub.

Step 1: In VS Code, click "Terminal" at the top menu, then "New Terminal". A text panel will open at the bottom of the screen.

Step 2: Type the following commands, pressing Enter after each one:

```
git init
git add .
git commit -m "Initial project setup"
```

Step 3: Go back to your GitHub webpage. Look for the section titled "...or push an existing repository from the command line". Copy the first line (it will look something like git remote add origin https://github.com/yourname/seatsync-monorepo.git).

Step 4: Paste that copied line into your VS Code terminal and press Enter.

Step 5: Finally, type this command and press Enter:

```
git push -u origin main
```

Congratulations. You have officially created your local project, initiated version control, and securely backed it up to your private cloud repository.

5. Installing the Engines (Node.js)

Concept

Computers do not inherently understand the programming languages we use to build websites. They need an "engine" or a "runtime environment" to translate our human-readable code into machine instructions. Since SeatSync uses a modern React framework for the frontend, we need an engine capable of running JavaScript outside of a web browser.

This engine is called Node.js. It comes paired with a tool called npm (Node Package Manager), which is essentially an app store for developers. It allows you to download pre-written packets of code to speed up your development.

Example

If your code is a DVD, Node.js is the DVD player. Without the player, the disc is just a piece of plastic. You need to install the player so your computer can execute the software.

Action Steps

Step 1: Go to nodejs.org.

Step 2: You will see two large download buttons. Always choose the one labeled "LTS" (Long Term Support). This is the stable, reliable version.

Step 3: Run the downloaded installer.

Step 4: Click "Next" through the prompts. Accept the license agreement. Leave the default installation folder as is.

Step 5: Keep clicking "Next" and then "Install." You do not need to check the box about installing tools for native modules right now.

Step 6: Click "Finish". Node.js and its companion, npm, are now installed on your system.

6. Initializing your frontend on your local PC

Use following example prompt to get instructions to initialize your Node.js environment:

You are an experienced Application Infrastructure Engineer. I have following folder structure for my SeatSync Web App on my windows PC:

seatsync-monorepo/
├── .github/workflows/ (Automated CI/CD deployment scripts)
├── frontend-web/ (React/Next.js code - deployed to Vercel)
├── Python-tools/ (Python Tool / future python components)
├── database/ (Supabase SQL migration files, Edge Functions)
└── core-artifacts/ (Documentations: Core Blueprint, Interface Contracts)

I have installed VS Code on PC. We plan to use React/Next.js and Supabase dev project in the cloud for our backend Postgres database.

Please provide me step by step instructions to initialize React/Next.js and set up the environment (.env) configuration required to connect to my Dev Supabase environment. My front-end code will be deployed to a QA and Prod environments in Vercel.

Make the instructions simple and brief in checklist format.

Example content of .env file:

```
# Connect to Supabase
NEXT_PUBLIC_SUPABASE_URL=https://xxxxxxxxxxxxxxxx.supabase.co
NEXT_PUBLIC_SUPABASE_ANON_KEY=xxxxxxxxxxxxxxxxxxxxxxxxxxxx
x
SUPABASE_SERVICE_ROLE_KEY=xxxxxxxxxxxxxxxxxxxxxxxxxxxxxxxxxx
xxx
```

# We will add Stripe keys here
NEXT_PUBLIC_STRIPE_PUBLISHABLE_KEY=pk_live_xxxxxxxxxxxxxxxxxxxxxxxxxx
STRIPE_SECRET_KEY=sk_live_xxxxxxxxxxxxxxxxxxxxxxxxxxxxxxxxxxxxxxxx
STRIPE_WEBHOOK_SECRET=whsec_xxxxxxxxxxxxxxxxxxxxxxxxxxxxxxxxxxxxxxxxxx

Store similar keys for the Quality Assurance and Production environments in encrypted Vercel Environment Variable and not in GitHub.

7. Installing the Engines (Python)

Concept

While Node.js handles our frontend website and backend call functions. We decided earlier in our architecture we will use Supabase Edge Functions. We will install Python. Many of your own project may require it. Also, Python is excellent for writing small tools for support activities. In Appendix B we have used Python to write a simple tool to analyze your token usage.

Python is renowned for its readability and massive ecosystem, making it excellent for processing data, building data pipelines and integrating AI services.

Just like Node.js, Python requires its own runtime engine to be installed on your local machine so it can understand the backend code when you add it.

Example

If Node.js is an English translator handling customer service at the front desk, Python is the accountant in the back office who speaks Spanish. Your business (the computer) needs to hire both translators to operate efficiently.

Action Steps

Step 1: Go to python.org/downloads.

Step 2: Click the large yellow button that says "Download Python". (It will usually display the latest stable version, like 3.12).

Step 3: Open the installer. CRITICAL STEP: Before you click "Install Now," look at the very bottom of the installer window. You MUST check the box that says "Add Python to PATH." If you miss this, your computer will not know where to find Python when we try to run it later.

Step 4: Once that box is checked, click "Install Now".

Step 5: Wait for the setup to complete, and click "Close".

8. Adding a Simple Test Code File

Concept

You have gathered your tools and set up your workspace. Now it is time to verify that everything is functioning correctly. In software development, it is standard practice to create a "Hello World" test file. This is the simplest possible piece of code used to confirm that your engines are running and your environment is properly configured.

We will write a tiny JavaScript program that creates a local web server.

Example

This is like turning the key in the ignition of a newly built car just to make sure the engine turns over. We aren't driving on the highway yet; we just want to hear the engine purr.

Action Steps

Step 1: Open VS Code (if you closed it). Ensure your seatsync-monorepo is open in the Explorer panel on the left.

Step 2: Right-click on your frontend-web folder and select "New File...".

Step 3: Name the file exactly server.js and press Enter.

Step 4: The empty server.js file will open in the main editor window. Carefully copy and paste the following block of code exactly as it appears below into the file:

```
const http = require('http');
const hostname = '127.0.0.1';
const port = 3000;

const server = http.createServer((req, res) => {
  res.statusCode = 200;
  res.setHeader('Content-Type', 'text/plain');
  res.end('Workspace configured successfully! The engine is
running.');
});

server.listen(port, hostname, () => {
  console.log(`Server running at http://${hostname}:${port}/`);
});
```

Step 5: Save the file. You can do this by going to File > Save, or by pressing Ctrl + S (Windows) or Cmd + S (Mac).

9. Launching Your Local Server

Concept

Your test code is written, but it is currently dormant. To bring it to life, we must instruct Node.js to execute the file. By doing so, we create a "Localhost" server. Localhost simply means "this computer." Port 3000 is a specific communication channel on your machine. Think of it like a specific radio frequency. We are going to broadcast our mini-website locally on frequency 3000.

Example

Usually, when you visit a website like Google, your browser travels across the internet to fetch data from a server far away. With localhost, your browser fetches data from a server running directly on your own hard drive. It is a closed loop, perfect for private testing before sharing your app with the world.

Action Steps

Step 1: In VS Code, look at the terminal panel at the bottom of the screen. If it is closed, click Terminal > New Terminal from the top menu.

Step 2: Right now, your terminal is pointing to the root of your project (seatsync-monorepo). Since our test file is inside the frontend-web folder, we need to navigate there. Type the following command and press Enter:

cd frontend-web

Note 4: *"cd" stands for Change Directory. You have just stepped inside the frontend folder.*

Step 3: Now, tell your Node.js engine to run the file. Type this command and press Enter:

node server.js

Step 4: If you did everything correctly, the terminal will print a message that says:

Server running at http://127.0.0.1:3000/

Step 5: The final test. Open your web browser (Chrome, Edge, or Safari). In the address bar at the very top, type:

localhost:3000

Step 6: Press Enter. Your browser should load a plain white page displaying the text: "Workspace configured successfully! The engine is running."

Clean up after the test

We want to leave our Monorepo in a pristine state do following to remove the test file:

1. In the Visual Studio terminal enter CTRL + C to kill the server process.
2. Using windows explorer go to folder C:\seatsync-monorepo\frontend-web, select the file ***server.js*** and press delete.

Now you are ready to build in chapter 11.

Conclusion

Take a moment to celebrate. You have just completed one of the most daunting hurdles for any new software creator. You have transformed a standard computer into a professional development environment.

To stop your server, go back to your VS Code terminal and press Ctrl + C. This shuts down the engine, freeing up port 3000.

Your monorepo is established, your version control is tracking changes, your codebase is safely backed up to GitHub, and your runtime engines are installed and verified. In the next chapter, we will begin exploring the UI design systems that will make up the visual layer of the SeatSync application.

A Note from your mentor on frustration

As we proceed deeper into the technical build in upcoming chapters, you will invariably encounter moments where something does not work on the first try. Perhaps a comma is missing in your code, or a folder was misnamed. This is entirely normal. Even the most seasoned engineers spend a significant portion of their day debugging errors.

When you hit a roadblock, take a deep breath. Re-read the error messages in your VS Code terminal—they are usually trying to tell you exactly where the problem lies. The workspace you have just constructed is safe. Because of Git and GitHub, you cannot permanently break your project. You have an several safety nets. Proceed with confidence.

If you are using Mac or Ubuntu

Copy our above instructions for windows and paste it in your AI prompt telling it to give you the equivalent steps for Mac or Ubuntu. You should have all you need to set up your local environment.

It's time to choose your AI coding platform.

You can choose Gemini, Claude or ChatGPT , but make it a paid subscription. It is very hard to complete a real project on a free tier. For the research for this book I used a paid version of Gemini and also used free versions of ChatGPT and MS Copilot and Grok for clarifying questions or 'second opinions'. This kept my main coding chat shorter and reduced hallucination.

Chapter 9: The Art of the Coding Prompt

Treating the AI like a magic wand does not work. If you type, "Build me a secure dashboard that shows user data and looks modern," hit enter, and wait for a miracle, you will get broken code, hallucinated libraries, and a massive headache. You might think the AI was flawed. In reality, your prompting was flawed. You need to know 'AI speak'.

Having deep dived in transformers and LLMs I can tell you a fundamental truth: *Large Language Models (LLMs) are hyper-advanced probability engines.* When you ask an LLM a question, it is calculating the most mathematically probable next word based on billions of parameters. If your prompt is vague, the probability space is massive. The AI has to guess what you mean, and in software engineering, guessing leads to critical bugs.

In this chapter, we transition from theory to practice. You have your Core Blueprint and your design artifacts. Now, it is time to write code. But you will not be typing syntax. You will be engineering prompts. I will share specialized techniques that professional AI engineers use to *constrain the model, narrow the probability space, and generate production-ready code* with near-perfect accuracy.

The Anatomy of a Perfect Code-Generation Prompt

A perfect code-generation prompt is not a polite request; it is a strict mathematical constraint. To get perfect code, your prompt must contain four specific anatomical parts:

The Persona,

The Context,

The Intent,

and The Output Format.

Raw LLM token sampling is non-deterministic, contextual prompt boundaries drastically reduce the variance space, transforming random token prediction into a controllable execution pipeline.

Concept: The Four Pillars of a Coding Prompt

Let us break down exactly how to structure your commands:

1. *The Persona*: *LLMs act differently depending on who they think they are.* By assigning a persona, you force the AI to access the highest-quality subset of its training data. Never just ask a question. Always start with, 'Act as an expert Senior [Language] Developer.'
2. *The Context*: The AI knows nothing about your app until you tell it. This is where you inject your Core Design Artifacts (from Chapter 5) and the specific file you are working on.
3. *The Intent*: What exactly do you want the AI to do? This must be microscopic in focus. Do not ask for a feature; ask for a function.
4. *The Output Format*: A specialized secret in AI engineering is *'Deterministic Forcing.'* You must tell the AI exactly how to print the answer. If you don't, it will output conversational fluff, which wastes your token budget and breaks your code.

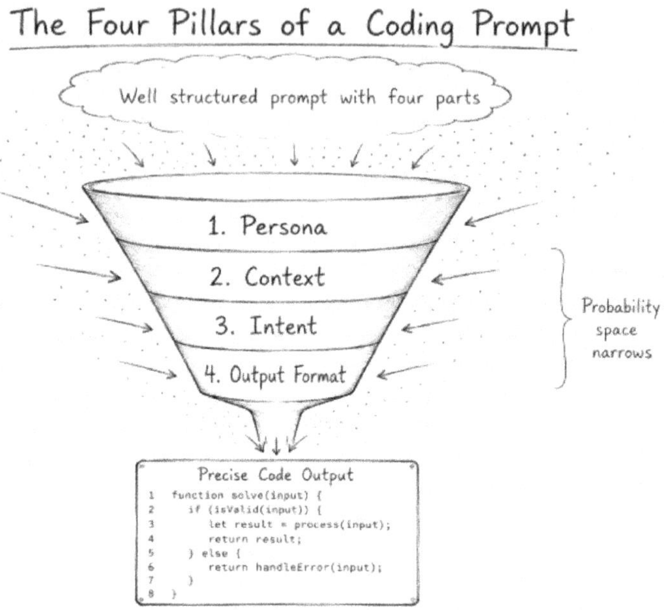

Fig 9-1

Example: The Vague Prompt vs. The Engineered Prompt

Let's look at SeatSync. We need to write the code that connects the front-end reservation button to the back-end database.

THE VAGUE PROMPT (High probability of failure):

> *"Write a function that lets a user book a seat in the app."*

Why this fails: The AI doesn't know what database you are using, what the user data looks like, or what language to write it in. It will guess, and it will guess wrong.

THE ENGINEERED PROMPT (High probability of success):

> *Act as a Senior TypeScript and Supabase Developer.*

CONTEXT:
[PASTE INTERFACE CONTRACT HERE]
We are working on the 'bookSeat' function in the 'ReservationService.ts' file.

INTENT:
Write a TypeScript asynchronous function that accepts a 'userId' and a 'shopId'. It must insert a new row into the 'Reservations' table in Supabase. It must handle errors if the database is offline.

OUTPUT FORMAT:
Output ONLY the raw TypeScript code block. Do not include any conversational text or explanations before or after the code.

Action Steps: Mastering the Anatomy

- Create a basic text template on your computer with the headers: *PERSONA, CONTEXT, INTENT, OUTPUT FORMAT.*
- For every major coding task, fill out this template before pasting it into the AI chat.
- Always end your code-generation prompts with the phrase: *'Output ONLY the code block.* No conversational filler.' This saves massive amounts of tokens.

Iterative Prompting: The Step-by-Step Method

One of the secrets of prompt engineering is a concept called *'Chain of Thought.' LLMs are much smarter when they are allowed to think step-by-step.* If you ask an AI to write an entire mobile app in one prompt, its internal attention mechanism collapses under the weight of the complexity.

Concept: The Illusion of the Whole App

You must never ask the AI to build a whole feature at once. Instead, you build a 'skeleton' first, and then you ask the AI to fill in the organs one by one. I call this *'Skeleton Prompting.'* By establishing the structure first, the AI has a rigid framework to operate within, severely limiting its ability to hallucinate by limiting its probability space.

Example: Skeleton Prompting for SeatSync

Instead of asking the AI to write the entire checkout flow for SeatSync, we break it down iteratively.

Step 1: The Skeleton Prompt

Example Prompt: *Act as a Senior Node.js/TypeScript backend developer. I am building the checkout module for my web app SeatSync. I do not want you to write the logic yet. I only want you to write the 'skeleton' of a class with empty functions, docstrings explaining what each function will do, and the necessary imports. Output only the skeleton code.*

The AI will output something like this:

```
/**
 * CheckoutService
 * Skeleton class for handling SeatSync checkout workflow.
 * All methods are intentionally left without logic.
 */
```

```
export class CheckoutService {
  private stripe: Stripe;

  constructor(stripeSecretKey: string) {
    /**
     * Initialize Stripe client with the provided secret key.
     */
    this.stripe = new Stripe(stripeSecretKey, { apiVersion:
'2024-06-20' });
  }
```

Step 2: The Iterative Meat Prompt

Now, we target a single function within that skeleton.

> Example Prompt: *Now we will write the logic for '* ***CheckoutService****. Here is the skeleton we are working with: [Paste Skeleton]. Using the Stripe API documentation for Type Script , write ONLY the code inside the 'CheckoutService' function. Handle network errors gracefully.*

By feeding the skeleton back to the AI, it knows exactly where its new code fits into the larger picture. It won't invent a new class. It won't forget the imports. It acts like a laser-guided missile.

Action Steps: Iterative Execution

- Ask the AI to generate a list of code files that will need to solve the problem.
- Always ask the AI to generate a 'skeleton' or 'outline' of the code file first.

- Review the skeleton to ensure the logic matches your Core Blueprint.
- Prompt the AI to write the functions one by one, constantly reminding it of the overarching skeleton.

Embedding Core Philosophies into Base Prompts

As a solo founder, you are responsible for *Security, Privacy, and Simplicity*. The problem is that LLMs were trained on the internet. A lot of the code on the internet is insecure, overly complex, and leaks data. If you don't explicitly tell the AI to be secure, it will often default to the easiest, most common (and therefore vulnerable) code path.

Concept: The Foundational System Prompt

To counter this, we use a *'Foundational System Prompt.'* This is a master set of instructions that you place at the very beginning of every new chat window (alongside your Core Design Artifacts). It fundamentally alters the weights of the AI's generation, forcing it to prioritize your core philosophies above all else.

Example: The SeatSync Foundation Prompt

When spinning up a new Virtual Team chat, we use this prompt before asking for any code:

> *You are the Lead Back-End Engineer for SeatSync. Before we write any code, you must adopt these unbreakable rules:*
> *1. SECURITY FIRST: Never trust user input. Always sanitize data before it hits the database. Prevent SQL injection and Cross-Site Scripting by default.*

2. PRIVACY FIRST: We collect minimal data. Never log plain-text passwords or personally identifiable information (PII) to the console.
3. SIMPLICITY: Reject clever, complex code. Write boring, readable code. If a one-line solution is hard to read, write it in three readable lines.
Do you acknowledge these constraints? Reply only 'ACKNOWLEDGED' if you understand.

Once the AI acknowledges this, its *probability engine is primed.* When it goes to write a database query, it will automatically wrap it in a prepared statement (a security best practice) because the concept of 'SECURITY FIRST' is actively weighting its neural network.

The AI Engineering best practice: Constraining Refactoring

I will leave you with one of the most frustrating aspects of AI coding and how to solve it. Often, you will ask the AI to fix a bug on line 45 of your code. The AI will fix the bug, but it will also 'helpfully' rewrite lines 1 through 44, changing variable names and breaking things that were already working.

Fig 9-2

Concept: Boundary Forcing

LLMs love to refactor. To stop this, you must use ***Boundary Forcing***. You tell the AI exactly what it is NOT allowed to touch.

Example: The Boundary Prompt

> *I have a bug in the 'calculate_total' function. Here is the entire file. I want you to fix the bug in 'calculate_total'.*
> *CRITICAL INSTRUCTION: You are forbidden from modifying any other function in this file. Do not change my variable names. Do not refactor my imports.*
> *Output ONLY the updated 'calculate_total' function, and nothing else.*

Summary and Next Steps

Prompt engineering for code is not like talking to a human; it is about programming a highly complex probability machine. By mastering the Anatomy of a Prompt, utilizing Skeleton Prompting, and embedding your Core Philosophies, you transition from a frustrated founder to a master Systems Architect.

Your Action Steps Before Chapter 10:

1. Set up your text expander or a notepad file with the Persona, Context, Intent, Output Format template.
2. Save the 'Foundational System Prompt' detailing your security and simplicity rules.
3. Practice taking a large problem and breaking it down into a 'Skeleton Prompt' first.

We are now ready to unleash these exact prompting techniques on our infrastructure. In Chapter 10, we will officially spin up the Back-End and Database Virtual Teams and start bringing the data logic of our application to life.

Chapter 10: Building the Back-End and Database

A startup had built a gorgeous user interface. Their marketing was brilliant, and their launch day brought in ten thousand eager users. Within two hours, the entire application collapsed. The problem wasn't the code on the user's screen; it was the foundation. Their database was essentially a glorified spreadsheet acting as a NoSQL bucket, with no indexes, no relational constraints, and security loopholes wide enough to drive a truck through. They lost half their user base on day one.

Experienced Database Architects who builds systems on PostgreSQL, MS SQL, and modern cloud infrastructures see this constantly. Non-technical founders often rush to build what they can see—the front-end buttons and screens. But the true value of your software, and the true safety of your users, lives in the back-end.

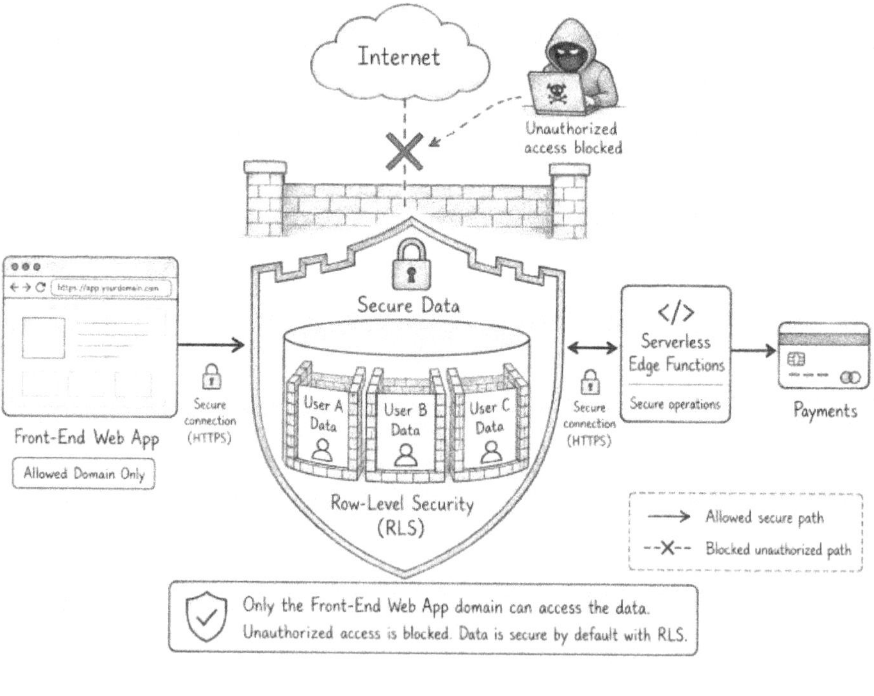

Fig 10-1

In this chapter, we are going to spin up your Database and Back-End Virtual Teams. I am going to share my knowledge and experience on how to deduce the perfect database structure from a simple application description. We will learn how to prompt the AI to define tables, build relationships, optimize with indexes, and enforce strict security policies by default. Finally, we will generate a *condensed Database Architecture Document* that your front-end team will use as their North Star.

Spinning Up Your Database Virtual Team

In traditional development, the Database Administrator (DBA) and the Back-End Engineer are often different roles, or at least different hats worn by a senior developer. The DBA ensures data is stored safely, efficiently, and logically. The Back-End Engineer writes the API (Application Programming Interface) logic that safely retrieves that data and hands it to the front-end.

For our purposes, we will treat the Database and Back-End as a unified "Back-End Virtual Team" in your AI chat. But we must sequence our prompts carefully: we architect the database first, and then we write the API logic.

Concept: The Initialization Prompt

To get the highest quality architecture, you must assign the AI the persona of an elite Database Architect. You need the AI to think in terms of strict data types, relational integrity, and security.

Example: Initializing the Team

Open a fresh chat window. Do not bring in the baggage from your previous brainstorming sessions. Paste this exact prompt:

Act as an elite Database Architect and Senior Back-End Developer. Your expertise lies in PostgreSQL, Supabase, and secure cloud infrastructure. I am the solo founder.

We are going to build the back-end for my application in Supabase. Before we begin, you must agree to my core philosophies:
1. Security by Default: We will use Row-Level Security (RLS) and strict authentication. Never trust user input.
2. Relational Integrity: We will use strict foreign keys and appropriate indexing for scalability.
3. Simplicity: We will avoid overly complex schemas.

I will provide the Core Blueprint next. Do you acknowledge your role and these constraints? Reply 'ACKNOWLEDGED' and ask for the Blueprint.

Action Steps
1. Open your AI tool and start a new chat titled 'Back-End & DB Team'.
2. Paste the Initialization Prompt.
3. Once the AI acknowledges, paste the 'Core Blueprint' and 'Data Logic Contract' artifacts you generated in Chapter 5.

Deducing the Database Architecture
Once the AI has your Core Blueprint, it needs to translate your business rules into a database structure. A good architect can look at a minimal description of a SaaS product and instantly deduce the required entities (tables), relationships, and data types.
Concept: Entities, Relationships, and Data Types
Let's define a few technical terms simply:
Entities (Tables): The nouns in your application. If you have Users, Coffee Shops, and Reservations, those are your three tables.
Relationships (Foreign Keys): How the nouns interact. A Reservation belongs to one User and one Coffee Shop. We

enforce this using Foreign Keys, which prevent a reservation from existing if the user is deleted.
Data Types: The strict format of a column. Is it a number (Integer), text (VARCHAR), a true/false flag (Boolean), or a timestamp? Picking the right data type saves immense amounts of server memory and speeds up searches.
Primary Keys (UUIDs): Every row in a table needs a unique identifier. Instead of using 1, 2, 3 (which hackers can easily guess to steal data), modern apps use UUIDs (Universally Unique Identifiers), which look like long strings of random characters.

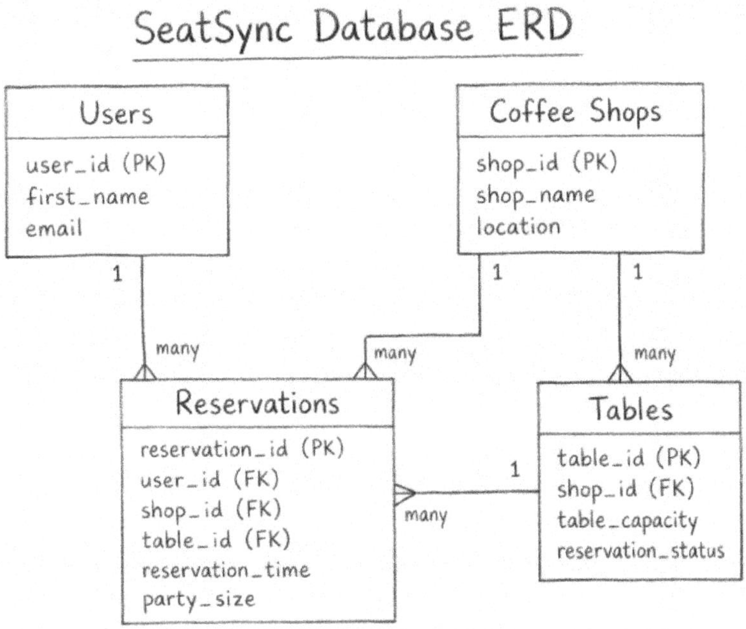

Fig 10-2: Entity Relationship Diagram

Example: Prompting for the Schema
With the AI primed, you ask it to design the exact structure for our SeatSync app. Notice how we ask clarifying questions to ensure the AI doesn't make assumptions.

Based on the SeatSync Blueprint, determine the complete PostgreSQL database structure required. For each table,

provide:
1. The table name.
2. The columns, their strict data types (prefer UUID for primary keys, TIMESTAMPTZ for dates), and column sizes.
3. The foreign key relationships.
4. Required indexes to make querying fast (e.g., indexing foreign keys).
5. Clarifying questions if the business logic is ambiguous.
Output this as a structured list, not SQL code yet.

The AI will output a beautifully structured design. For the Reservations table, it will specify a UUID for the ID, a 'user_id' referencing the Users table, and 'start_time' and 'end_time' as timestamps. It will also explicitly tell you to index the 'shop_id' column because users will frequently search for reservations by coffee shop.

Action Steps
1. Ask the AI to deduce the schema based on your Blueprint.
2. Review the proposed tables. Are there any missing 'nouns' from your app?
3. Ensure the AI has included indexes on columns that will be searched frequently.

Security Conscious Design: Authentication and RLS
We are building on a modern cloud database like Supabase or AWS. These platforms are incredibly powerful, but if you do not lock the doors, your data is public. As a security-conscious architect, never build a table without building the moat around it.

Concept: Authentication vs. Authorization
These two terms sound similar but are vastly different:
Authentication (AuthN): Who are you? This is the process of a user logging in with an email/password or Google Single Sign-On. The system issues them a cryptographic badge called a JWT (JSON Web Token).

Authorization (AuthZ): What are you allowed to do? Just because you are logged in doesn't mean you can delete someone else's reservation.

Concept: Row-Level Security (RLS)
In PostgreSQL, we use *Row-Level Security (RLS).* RLS acts as a bouncer at the database level. Even if a hacker breaches your API, the database itself will reject the query if the user's JWT token doesn't match the row they are trying to access. It is the gold standard for SaaS privacy.

Example: Prompting for RLS Policies
Once you approve the table structure, you must prompt the AI to write the SQL script to generate the database and enforce these policies.

I approve the table structure. Now, generate the full SQL script to create these tables in Supabase Postgres.
CRITICAL INSTRUCTION: You must include SQL commands to enable Row-Level Security (RLS) on every single table.
Write the RLS policies so that:
- A user can only view and delete their OWN reservations.
- A user can only view their OWN profile.
- Anyone logged in can view the Coffee Shops table, but only an admin can edit it.
Include comments in the SQL explaining the security policies.

Action Steps
1. Never accept a database generation script that does not include RLS policies.
2. Clearly define in plain English who is allowed to Read, Insert, Update, and Delete data in each table.
3. Run the generated SQL script in your cloud database provider's SQL editor (like the Supabase dashboard).

Prompting for Secure Server Logic (API Endpoints)

Now that your database exists and is locked down, you need a way for your front-end (the user's screen) to safely talk to it. This is done through *API Endpoints*—the messengers.
If you chose a platform like Supabase or Firebase, the APIs are actually auto-generated for you based on your tables! However, you will often need custom server logic for things the database shouldn't do alone—like charging a credit card via Stripe or sending a confirmation email.

Concept: Edge Functions and Serverless Architecture
To keep our Low-Cost and Scalability philosophies intact, we use *Serverless Functions* (or *Edge Functions*). Instead of paying for a server that runs 24/7, you write a small snippet of *TypeScript (Deno)*. The cloud provider only runs this code—and only charges you—when a user clicks a button.

Example: Prompting for an Edge Function
Let's say SeatSync needs to charge the user when they book a seat. You cannot do this securely on the front-end; a user could easily manipulate the code to change the price to zero. It must happen on the back-end.

We need to write a serverless Edge Function in TypeScript (Deno) for Supabase.
INTENT: Create an endpoint called 'process-payment'. It receives a 'user_id', 'shop_id', and 'amount'.
SECURITY: It must verify the user's JWT token. It must call the Stripe API to process the payment. If the payment succeeds, it inserts a record into the 'Reservations' table using the Supabase Admin client.
Use 'Skeleton Prompting' first. Give me the outline of the function and imports, and wait for my approval before writing the logic.

For simple task you can use a single prompt to generate the required code file. For complex code files with several functions use our 'Skeleton Prompting technique' from Chapter 9, you ensure the AI includes all the necessary security checks (like verifying the JWT token) before it gets bogged down in the complex Stripe API logic.

Action Steps

1. Identify the actions in your app that require absolute security (payments, sending emails, complex calculations).
2. Prompt the AI to write these as Serverless Functions.
3. Always explicitly command the AI to verify the user's authentication token at the very beginning of the function code.

Generating the Core Artifact: The Database Architecture Document

You have now built a robust, relational, highly secure database and written the server logic to support it. But remember the Context Economy from Chapter 5? Your AI chat window is now filling up with SQL code, Stripe API discussions, and RLS policies.

Before we move to Chapter 11 and spin up the Front-End Virtual Team, *we need to extract the 'state' of the database. We need a condensed, highly technical design document that explains exactly how to talk to this database. This becomes the Interface Contract.*

Concept: The Interface Contract

The front-end doesn't care how the Stripe API works. It only cares about what data it needs to send, and what data it will get back. The Interface Contract summarizes this.

Example: Prompting for the Contract

Use this 'Shrink Ray' prompt to finalize the Back-End chat:

We have successfully built the database and API. I need you to generate a condensed 'Database Architecture Document' for consumption by the Front-End Virtual Team.
It must include:
1. A brief summary of the tables and their exact column names/types.

2. The specific API endpoints available (e.g., 'process-payment'), the exact JSON payload required, and the expected response.
3. Zero conversational fluff. Use strict technical notation. Output this as a markdown code block so I can save it.

Save this document immediately. It is the crucial bridge that will allow your front-end code to seamlessly integrate with your new database without hallucination or friction.

Summary and Next Steps
You have successfully acted as an elite Database Architect. You didn't just throw data into a bucket; you designed a robust relational schema. You prioritized Security by Default by implementing Row-Level Security, ensuring that user data is walled off from bad actors. You leveraged Serverless Edge Functions to handle secure operations like payments, keeping your infrastructure lean and low-cost.

Your Action Steps Before Chapter 11:
1. Initialize your Back-End & DB Team chat using the expert persona.
2. Prompt for the schema, review the data types and indexes, and generate the SQL script.
3. Run the SQL script in your cloud provider (like Supabase) to physically create the database.
4. Generate the condensed Database Architecture Document and save it locally.

With the foundation poured and the security moats dug, we get to move to the part of the project that your users will actually see. In next chapter we will take our Core Artifacts, spin up the Front-End Virtual Team, and build a beautiful, responsive user interface.

Chapter 11: Building the Front-End

Here is a story of a startup, whose application front-end had a flawed architecture. Their user interface was stunning—smooth animations, beautiful typography, and a seamless mobile design. The founders were thrilled. But on launch day, with just three hundred concurrent users, the entire application froze, and the database crashed.

Digging into the code they found the culprit. Every time a user typed a single letter into the search bar, the front-end fired a request to the database. Three hundred users typing ten letters each meant three thousand database requests per second. The UI was pretty, but the architecture was fundamentally naive. They had ignored network round-trips and state management.

Any experienced Front-End Architect will tell you that the UI is not just a coat of paint. It is the intelligent bridge between human intent and server logic. A poorly designed front-end will bankrupt your server costs, expose private data, and consume your entire token budget in debugging.

In this chapter, we will spin up your *Front-End Virtual Team*. We will recall the decisions we made in Chapter 4: we are building a Progressive Web App (PWA) optimized for mobile screens, using React (Next.js) and Tailwind CSS for the front-end, connecting to Supabase database. I will guide you through a series of architectural questions that will force the AI to design a scalable, low-cost, and configurable user interface. Finally, we will generate the UI Architecture Document—the ultimate artifact for this phase of the build.

The Golden Rule: Dev vs. QA vs. Prod Environments

Before we write a single line of interface code, we must establish our infrastructure boundary. One of the most dangerous things a solo founder can do is test new code on the live database where real users are interacting with the app.

Concept: Multiple parallel Infrastructure
You must build three completely separate versions of your application: *Dev environment* on your PC, *Quality Assurance* (QA) and *Production* (Prod) in cloud.

Dev: This is environment on your PC your codes in here first for testing. However to make things simple your database will be on Supabase 'seatsync-dev'. You won't need a corresponding Vercel environment your desktop React/Next.js will suffice.

Quality Assurance (QA): This is your playground. You have a 'seatsync-qa' Supabase database and QA Vercel hosting project. You use fake, generated data here. If you break the database schema, it does not matter. This is where your AI virtual teams operate. This is where you run your ' test suites'. All your tests must pass and your application must work like a 'symphony' here before you push the code to production.

The Prod Environment: This is the sacred, live version of your app. 'seatsync-prod'. This where your customers are using your system. You only push code to Vercel Prod after you have clicked through the Dev and QA version yourself and verified there are no bugs. This is one of the practices we import from the 'old world' of software engineering into our new world of AI coding. By enforcing this separation, you adhere to our Security philosophy. You ensure that half-finished AI-generated code never accidentally drops a real user's reservation.

Spinning Up the Front-End Virtual Team
Just as we did with the database, we need a dedicated chat conversation for the front-end. This chat must be completely isolated from your back-end chat to optimize your Context Memory. The front-end AI does not need to read the SQL scripts; it only needs to know the Interface Contract (the APIs) and the UI constraints.

Example: The UI Architect Initialization Prompt
Open a new AI chat window. Name it 'Front-End Team'. Start with this prompt to establish the persona and our core philosophies:

Act as a top-tier SaaS Front-End UI/UX Architect. Your expertise lies in building fast, beautiful, low-cost Progressive Web Apps (PWAs) using React (Next.js) and Tailwind CSS. I am the solo founder. We are building the front-end for our app, SeatSync.

You must strictly adhere to these principles:
1. Mobile-First PWA: The UI must feel like a native mobile app on a phone.
2. Network Optimization: We must minimize database I/O and network round trips using smart state management.
3. Configurable UI: Text, toggles, and feature flags should be driven by backend database configs, not hardcoded.
4. Simplicity: Reject complex CSS. Use standard Tailwind utility classes.

Do you acknowledge your role and constraints? Reply 'ACKNOWLEDGED', and I will provide the Database Architecture Document to begin our design.

Action Steps
1. Initialize the chat with the prompt above.
2. Once acknowledged, paste the Database Architecture Document from Chapter 10.
3. Keep this chat strictly for UI discussions. Do not ask it to write SQL/Backend code using this.

The UI Architecture Questionnaire
To build a robust front-end, we must not ask the AI to 'write the code.' We must first ask it to answer a series of

architectural questions. By guiding the AI through these specific inquiries, we build a comprehensive build map.

Question 1 & 2: Identifying Screens and Content
We need to know exactly how many user screens are required and what lives on them. A minimalist app keeps the screen count low.
Example Prompt:
Based on the architecture document, identify the absolute minimum number of user screens required for SeatSync to function. For each screen, detail the specific content (buttons, forms, lists) that will be displayed.

The AI should output a lean list: 1. Login/Signup Screen, 2. Home Dashboard (List of Shops), 3. Shop Details (Booking button), 4. My Reservations (List of active bookings).

Question 3: Code Files and Naming Conventions
Next, we map these screens to actual code files. A clean naming convention is vital for Context Memory. If you have a file named 'data_view_final_2.tsx', the AI will struggle. We want simple, predictable names.
Example Prompt:
Map these screens to Next.js file routes and reusable React components. Suggest a strict, simple naming convention for the UI code files (e.g., using PascalCase for components) and explain how they map to our back-end.

Question 4 & 5: Mapping the Backend APIs
The UI needs data. We must identify which frontend functions the UI will call, their purpose, inputs, and outputs.

Example Prompt:
List every data insert, update, delete functions the UI will need to consume. For each, define the purpose, the exact inputs the UI will send, and the expected output. Account for the 'process-payment' Edge Function on Supabase.

Question 6: Error Handling and Graceful Recovery
Networks fail. Users lose cell service while on the train. A beautiful UI must handle errors gracefully without showing a blank white screen.

Example Prompt:
Detail how the React application will handle errors. How do we implement Error Boundaries? How does the UI recover gracefully if the Supabase is unreachable? Detail exactly where client-side errors will be logged.

The AI will explain that client errors (like a failed React render) are caught by an Error Boundary component and can be logged to a free-tier service like Sentry, while database errors are logged securely in Supabase/.

Question 7: The Configurable UI
This is a hallmark of top-tier SaaS architecture. If you want to change the text on a button from 'Book Now' to 'Reserve Seat', you shouldn't have to rewrite code and redeploy the app. You should change a database field.

Example Prompt:
Explain how we will make the UI highly configurable. Suggest a 'ui_config' table in our database that the front-end fetches on load. What UI elements should be database-driven to make the app cheaper and easier to maintain without code deployments?

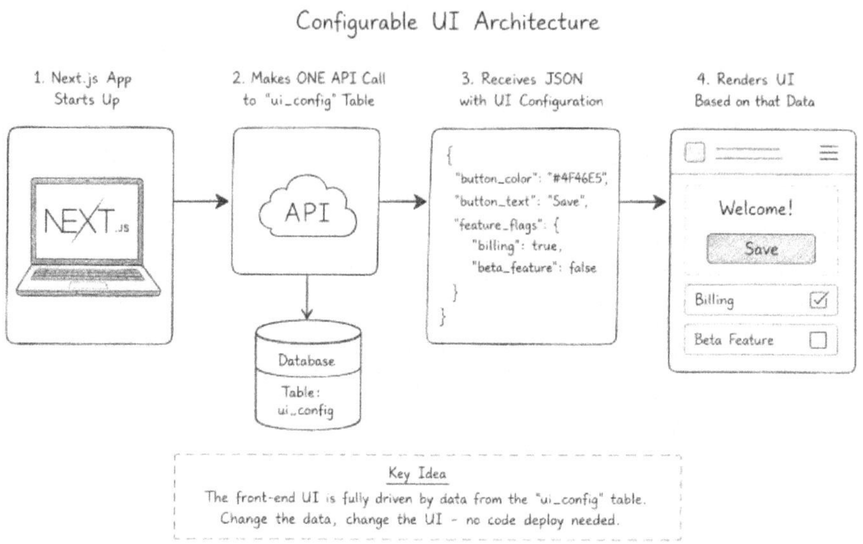

Fig 11-1

State Management and Network Optimization

Let us return to the story of the crashed database. To prevent that, *we must manage 'State' effectively*. State is simply the data the app remembers at any given moment (like what the user typed in a search bar).

Concept: Throttling, Debouncing, and Caching

To minimize database I/O (Input/Output) and network round trips, we use specific techniques:
Debouncing: If a user is typing a search term, the app waits until they stop typing for 300 milliseconds before sending the request to the database.
Caching: If the user views the 'Coffee Shops' list, we save that data in the browser's memory using a library like React Query or SWR. (Prompt your AI to get install instructions of these modules in your local Development environment before deployment to QA/Production.) If they navigate away and come back, we show the saved data instantly instead of asking the database again.

Example: Prompting for Network Optimization

For our 'Shop Details' and 'Search' screens, detail the state management strategy. We must minimize network round trips. Explain how we will implement debouncing for search inputs and caching for shop data to prevent database overload based on high concurrent users.

Generating the Core Artifact: The UI Architecture Document

You have now asked the right questions. The AI has provided the screens, the file names, the API mappings, the error handling, and the caching strategy.

Before we begin generating the actual React code, we must compress this knowledge. Just like we did in the back-end chapter, we need an artifact.

Example: The Artifact Generation Prompt

We have successfully designed the front-end architecture. Now, generate a concentrated 'UI Architecture Document'. It must be a dense, highly technical summary containing:

1. The exact Next.js file structure and component names.

2. The specific API mapping for each screen.

3. The state management and caching rules to minimize DB I/O.

4. The Configurable UI data model requirements.

Output this document with zero conversational filler. I will share this with the Database Team to see if we need to add new columns.

This document is a living blueprint. In fact, if the UI Architecture Document requires a 'ui_config' table, you now take this document, copy it, open your Back-End & DB Team chat, and say: 'The front-end requires a ui_config table. Please update the database schema and generate the SQL.' This is how your virtual teams communicate through you. They don’t call, email or text each other they use core design artifacts to communicate.

Connecting the Front-End to the Back-End APIs
With the document generated, it is time to write code. Because we are using Next.js and Supabase Edge Functions for secure server-side actions, while normal reads/writes go directly from Next.js to Supabase, the connection is straightforward via standard HTTPS fetch requests. But remember our Security philosophy: we must pass our authentication token securely.

Example: Code Generation for the API Call
When you are ready to have the AI write the component, use the Skeleton and Boundary prompting techniques from Chapter 6.
We are writing the 'ShopDetails.tsx' component.
INTENT: Write the React component that fetches the shop data from the backend.
SECURITY: You must include the user's Supabase JWT token in the Authorization header of the fetch request.
PERFORMANCE: Use React Query for caching to minimize network trips.
Output only the code block.

Use above prompt to generate the code for each code file identified for the Front-end using all the techniques shown in this book.

Summary and Next Steps
You have acted as a top-tier Front-End Architect. You established a strict Dev, QA, Prod environment to protect your live application. You guided the AI through a rigorous questionnaire to define screens, optimize network requests, handle errors gracefully, and make the UI configurable without constant redeployments.

Your Action Steps Before Chapter 12:
1. Create two separate environments in your hosting provider Vercel: one for QA, one for Prod. For Supabase your

database hosting environment create 3 environments. One each for Dev, QA and Production.
2. Spin up your Front-End Virtual Team chat and initialize the Architect persona.
3. Walk the AI through the UI questions: Screens, Files, Errors, and Configuration.
4. Generate the concentrated UI Architecture Document and save it. Cross-reference it with your Database chat to ensure all necessary tables exist.

You now have a fully architected application—business logic, database, and a mobile-optimized UI. In the next section we will stitch everything together to make application work in symphony.

Part V: The Launch – Bringing the Idea to Reality

Chapter 12: Integration and Quality Assurance

Welcome to the crucible. Up until this point, we have operated in isolated silos. You have architected your application, mastered the context economy, and managed your AI virtual teams to build the front-end components and the back-end logic. You have your React interface, and your Supabase database.

But a modern application is not a collection of isolated parts; it is well integrated , seamless communication between those parts. Brilliant codebases fail catastrophically because the integration was an afterthought. Security, scalability, high availability, and performance are not features you bolt on at the end—they are woven into the very fabric of how your systems talk to each other.

There is universal truth in software engineering: untested code is broken code. In the AI era, you are generating code at an unprecedented velocity. If your testing strategy does not scale with your generation velocity, you will be buried in *technical debt* before your first user signs up.

In this chapter, we will stitch the SeatSync application together. We will explore the physics of network communication, ensuring data is secure and latency is minimized. Then, we will turn our AI virtual teams into an automated QA department, prompting them to write test scripts and actively hunt for bugs in their own code.

The Architecture of Integration: Making Systems Talk

When your front-end (hosted on Vercel) needs to talk to your database (hosted on Supabase) via your serverless API, it must traverse the public internet. This journey is fraught with latency, security risks, and configuration mismatches. Application Infrastructure Integration is the art of making this journey as short, secure, and reliable as possible.

Concept: Geographic Co-Location and Network Physics

Data cannot travel faster than the speed of light. In reality it travels much slower. If your Vercel front-end is deployed in a data center in New York, and your Supabase database is hosted in Frankfurt, Germany, every single API request must cross the Atlantic Ocean. This introduces latency—often 250 to 500 milliseconds per round trip. If a simple page load requires five API calls, your user is waiting a full second just for network travel time. This is unacceptable for a modern app like SeatSync.

The solution is *Geographic Co-Location*. You must deploy your compute (front-end servers, edge functions) and your state (database) in the same geographic region. This is something you have to ensure when you are initially setting up the components/ projects in Vercel / Supabase / AWS/etc. Moving the instances after they have been created is complicated and difficult.

Example: Co-Locating SeatSync

When setting up SeatSync, you are prompted by Vercel and Supabase to choose a region. You do not leave this to default. You select 'us-east-1' (Northern Virginia) for your Supabase project. Consequently, when configuring Vercel, you ensure your Edge Functions are also deployed strictly to 'us-east-1' or a region physically adjacent to it. By doing this, the physical distance your data travels is reduced from thousands of miles to mere miles, dropping network latency to double-digit milliseconds.

Action Steps: Optimizing the Network Path

Step 1: Audit your infrastructure components. List out Vercel, Supabase, and any third-party APIs (like a payment gateway).
Step 2: Standardize the region. Choose a region closest to your primary user base (e.g., US-East, EU-Central) and force all providers into that region.
Step 3: Implement *Connection Pooling*. Serverless environments spin up thousands of micro-instances. If each creates a direct database connection, your database will crash. Use Supabase's built-in connection pooler (PgBouncer) to manage these connections efficiently.

Securing Data in Transit: The Zero-Trust Pipeline
Once the path is optimized, we must secure it. As an architect, my default stance is *'Zero Trust'*. You must assume that the network between Vercel and Supabase is actively hostile.

Concept: Environment Variables and Ephemeral Secrets
Never, under any circumstances, hardcode an API key, database password, or secret token into your source code. If your AI suggests a code snippet with a hardcoded secret—even for testing—reject it immediately. Going one step further I would suggest you make your GitHub code library private instead of public, this will give you another layer of protection against mistakes like uploading API keys to GitHub.
We secure data in transit using TLS/HTTPS (which Vercel and Supabase handle by default), but we secure access through Environment Variables. These are secure, hidden configurations injected into the server at runtime.

Example: Vercel to Supabase Handshake
Your React app needs to fetch seat availability from Supabase (database). The front-end uses the Supabase 'Anon Key' (safe to expose to the public, heavily restricted by Row-Level Security). Your backend serverless functions, however, need the 'Service Role Key' (bypasses all security, absolute power). You store the Service Role Key exclusively in Vercel's secure Environment Variable settings, absolutely inaccessible to the browser.

Action Steps: Establishing the Security Contract
Step 1: Create a `.env.local` file on your machine. Add your keys here. *Add `.env.local` to your `.gitignore` file immediately so it is never uploaded to GitHub.*
Step 2: Use the AI to generate a ***'Secrets Management Document'***—a simple list of which virtual team needs which key.
Step 3: Configure CORS (Cross-Origin Resource Sharing) on your backend API to explicitly only accept requests from your specific Vercel production domain (e.g., 'https://seatsync.com'), blocking requests from anywhere else.

Quality Assurance: The AI as Your QA Engineer
You have wired the systems together. They communicate quickly and securely. Now, we must ensure they actually work. In the past, writing tests was a tedious, labor-intensive process. Today, we utilize our AI as a dedicated QA Engineer.

Concept: The Automated Testing Pyramid
A robust testing strategy follows the *Testing Pyramid*. At the bottom, you have *Unit Tests* (testing a single function). In the middle, *Integration Tests* (testing the API talking to the database). At the top, End-to-End (E2E) Tests (simulating a user clicking through the app in a browser).
Because AI excels at pattern recognition and context processing, it is exceptionally good at writing all three layers, provided you give it the correct context—specifically, the ***Core Design Artifacts*** we generated in Chapter number 3.

Example: Prompting for SeatSync Unit Tests
Let's test the React component that displays available seats. Instead of writing the test manually, you provide the AI with the component code and ask it to generate tests using Jest and React Testing Library.

QA PROMPT - UNIT TESTING:
You are an expert QA Engineer. Below is the React component for the SeatSync 'SeatMap'.

[PASTE COMPONENT CODE]

Write a comprehensive suite of unit tests using Jest and React Testing Library.
Ensure you test:
1. The default state (loading spinner).
2. The success state (seats rendered correctly based on mock data).
3. The error state (handling a 500 response from the API).
Output only the test code. Use clean, descriptive block names.

Action Steps: Building the Test Suite
Step 1: Unit Tests (Frontend). Run the prompt above for all critical UI components. Run tests locally. If they fail, feed the error back to the AI for correction.
Step 2: Integration Tests (Backend). Provide your routing file to the AI and prompt it to *write 'Deno's native test runner (Deno.test)' or 'Jest integration specs'* that mock the Supabase database connection and test the functions request/response format.
Step 3: E2E Tests (Full Flow). Prompt the AI to write 'Playwright' or 'Cypress' scripts.

Example prompt: *'Write a Playwright script that navigates to the homepage, logs in with mock credentials, selects a coffee shop, and clicks the reserve seat button. Assert that the success toast appears.'*

Note 6: *If you are building a prototype and it is very small you can do manual testing initially. You do that by building a spreadsheet with all the tests you think that needs to be done. Whenever you move code to QA environment from Dev make sure you run all the tests. While for smaller project I don't want you to spend too much time building the automated test suite initially but you have to do it at some point. It gives you steady quality standard. As your SaaS code changes you will need to revisit your automated test suit and keep updating it to include new features. Last thing* *on this matter I will add do not only depend on your automated test scripts - you must have a human test it too.*

The Adversarial Paradigm: Forcing AI to Catch Its Own Bugs

The most dangerous bugs are the ones that pass all your tests because the tests were written with the same flawed logic as the code itself. *To break this echo chamber, we must change the AI's persona from 'Helpful Assistant' to 'Ruthless Adversary'.*

Concept: Adversarial Prompting

When an AI writes code, it tries to satisfy your immediate request. *It usually assumes a "happy path"*—where users click the right buttons and provide the correct data. Adversarial Prompting forces the AI to look at its own code through the lens of a hacker or a chaotic user trying to break the system.

Example: Auditing the Reservation Logic

You have completed the backend function that reserves a seat. Before deploying, you paste the code back into the AI with a very specific, aggressive prompt.
ADVERSARIAL PROMPT - SECURITY & LOGIC AUDIT:
You are a highly aggressive penetration tester and senior QA auditor. Review the following function for reserving a seat in SeatSync.

[PASTE CODE]

Your goal is to break this code.
1. Identify any race conditions (what if two users click reserve on the exact same millisecond?).
2. Identify any missing validation (what if the user sends a negative number for seat_id?).
3. Identify any security flaws (can a user reserve a seat for a different user?).
Do not rewrite the code yet. List the vulnerabilities in order of severity.

The AI will shift contexts. It might point out that while your code works perfectly for one user, it completely lacks a transaction lock, meaning two users could indeed double-book a seat. You have just saved yourself hours of production debugging.

Action Steps: The QA Checkpoint Protocol

Step 1: Before declaring any major feature complete, run an Adversarial Prompt against the backend logic and the database schema.

Step 2: Force the AI to audit edge cases. Ask: 'What happens if the user's internet drops immediately after clicking submit?'

Step 3: Implement the fixes suggested by the audit, then regenerate your Integration Tests to cover these newly discovered edge cases.

Conclusion

Integration and Quality Assurance are not the glamorous parts of building a product. They are the rigorous, disciplined systems that separate professional architectures from amateur weekend projects.

By intentionally co-locating your infrastructure to reduce latency, securing your transit with environment variables and strict CORS rules, and employing your AI as a dedicated, adversarial QA engineer, you build a fortress. You ensure that when SeatSync goes live, it will not crumble under the weight of real-world network traffic or malicious inputs.

The pieces are connected. The tests are green. The architecture is sound and secure. In Chapter 13, we will take the final leap. We will move from our local testing environments and launch into the cloud, exploring Continuous Integration, Continuous Deployment (CI/CD), and live production hosting.

Chapter 13: From Code to Cloud: Deployment

Up until now, your application has lived entirely as code files on your laptop and conceptual models inside your Virtual Teams' context windows. You have architected the system, mastered prompt engineering, built the front-end and back-end, and established rigorous Quality Assurance. But code on a laptop is a science project. To generate revenue, that code must live securely in the cloud where your customers can reach.

Deployment should be the most boring part of your day. The DevOps movement, which revolutionized software engineering over the past decade, relies heavily on automation. Human intervention during a deployment introduces errors. By automating the pipeline, we remove anxiety, ensure consistency, and allow founders to focus entirely on product innovation. A core principle of modern *DevOps* is deploying small, frequent changes rather than massive updates, which drastically reduces the risk of deployment errors. Software teams started deploying changes more frequently but in small numbers. This allowed teams to focus on each change and had a significant impact on reducing the number of errors per deployment. I would strongly recommend that you deploy few changes at a time instead of a large number of changes in one deployment.

AI generates code at an aggressive velocity. If your deployment process is manual and complex, it will become the ultimate bottleneck. In this chapter, we are going to spin up a new virtual team: The Infrastructure Team. We will structure your Git repository, reject overly complex local setups in favor of a pure cloud-first architecture, build separate deployment pipelines, and execute the exact workflow needed to take SeatSync live.

Note 7*: Having an automated deployment Continuous Integration (CI) \Continuous Deployment (CD) is your ultimate goal. However, if you are building a small prototype don't let this bog you down and delay your main* *product development. If your deployment steps are simple enough you can do this manually until you are ready.*

Keep in mind the automated deployments is the best practice in the software industry. If you are going to show case your product to a potential buyer you have to make sure you have already implemented CI/CD in your project.

The Code Structure: Organizing for Decoupled Teams
Before we can deploy your code, we must organize it. In Chapter 3, we established the need for separate Virtual Teams for the front-end and the back-end. Your Git repository must reflect this strict separation. Tangled code leads to tangled, failing deployments.

Concept: The Simplified Monorepo
A 'monorepo' (monolithic repository) means keeping all your project files in a single Git repository. For a solo founder, a well-structured monorepo is vastly superior for maintainability. The secret is absolute folder isolation. ***The front-end code must never reference files in any other folder***. They exist independently and communicate exclusively via network APIs.

Example: The SeatSync Repository Structure
Your local project folder should be structured exactly like this:

```
seatsync-monorepo/
├── .github/workflows/   (Automated CI/CD deployment scripts)
├── frontend-web/        (React/Next.js code - deployed to Vercel)
├── python-tools/        (Python tools)
├── database/            (Supabase SQL migration files)
└── core-artifacts/      (Your Core Blueprint, Interface Contracts)
```

Action Steps: Initializing Git
Step 1: Open your terminal and initialize the repository in your root folder using `*git init*`.

Step 2: Create the folder structure outlined above if you did not create it earlier in chapter .
Step 3: Enforce the boundary rule. When prompting the Front-End Virtual Team, explicitly forbid it from modifying any other directory. This isolates your *blast radius* during generation.

The Cloud-First Architecture: Redefining Environments
One should never deploy untested code directly to real users. To mitigate risk, we use multiple environments. Historically, this meant running complex tools like Docker on your local laptop to simulate a database.
I am going to advise you to completely reject that historical approach. Docker is resource-heavy, drains laptop batteries, and for a solo founder, troubleshooting local container networks is a frustrating waste of time. It violates our key design principle: Simplicity. In the AI era, where the machine is rapidly generating and testing SQL tables, we want instant feedback. We are going 100% cloud.

Concept: The Three-Tiered Cloud Strategy
We will create three identical, fully isolated cloud environments using Supabase and Vercel. For Vercel you will only need two environments , your PC will be the Dev environment for the Front-end. Supabase allows multiple free-tier projects, making this highly cost-effective.

1. *Development (SeatSync-Dev):* This is your private sandbox. The database lives in the cloud, but the frontend lives on your laptop and connects to it. When the AI generates a new database schema, you paste it directly into the Supabase web dashboard. It is instant, frictionless, and requires zero local server maintenance.

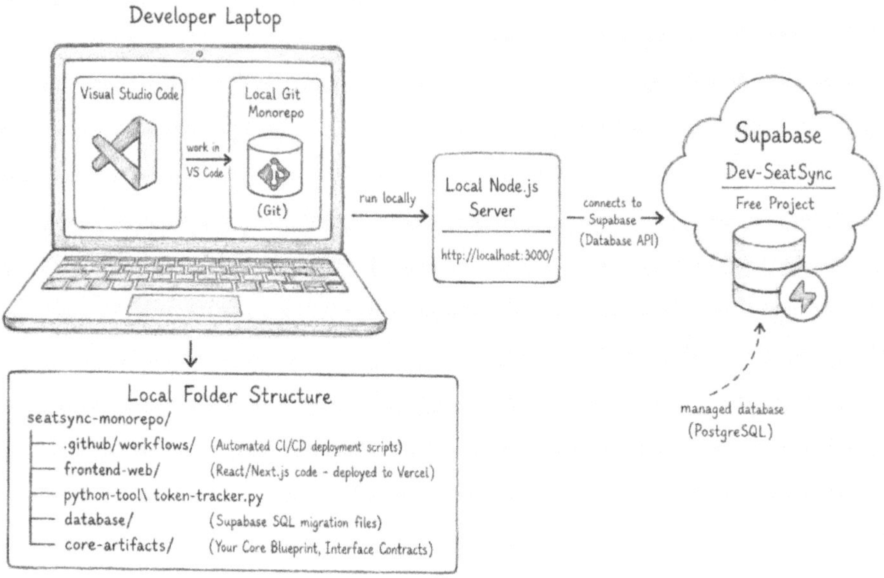

Fig 13-1: Development environment (same as Fig 8-1)

2. *Quality Assurance (SeatSync-QA):* This is your staging area. It runs on exact copies of your cloud infrastructure. It has a dedicated URL like `qa.seatsync.com`. You use this environment purely to test the full system integration, including third-party webhooks like Stripe's sandbox.
3. *Production (SeatSync-Prod):* This is the live, user-facing environment (`seatsync.com`). It is scaled for high availability, equipped with automated backups, and shielded from any experimental code.

Example: Why We Isolate Dev and QA
You might be tempted to use one database for both Dev and QA to save time. Do not do this. AI generation is a highly volatile laboratory. The AI will frequently suggest destructive SQL commands to test a new feature (e.g., `DROP TABLE users CASCADE;`). If Dev and QA share a database, a hallucinated query on your laptop will instantly corrupt the QA environment, breaking all your ongoing integration tests. Simplicity is good; shared blast radiuses are fatal. Keep them separated.

Action Steps: Standing up the Environments

Step 1: Create a free Supabase project named ***'SeatSync-Dev'***. Point your laptop's local `.env` file to this database. You test here.

Step 2: Create a second free Supabase project named ***'SeatSync-QA'***. Configure your `qa.seatsync.com` domain in Vercel and point it to this QA database.

Step 3: Create a third Supabase project named ***'SeatSync-Prod'*** (upgrade this one to the Pro tier for daily backups). Point your Vercel primary `seatsync.com` domain here.

Spinning up the Infrastructure Virtual Team

With our cloud environments ready, we must automate the delivery of code from your laptop to Vercel. We do this through Continuous Integration and Continuous Deployment (CI/CD) pipelines using GitHub Actions. We will spin up a new AI Virtual Team to write these scripts for us.

Concept: Two distinct pipelines (QA vs. Prod)

We do not want one massive, complex deployment script. We want two simple ones: `***deploy-qa.yml***` and `***deploy-prod***.yml`. The QA pipeline should be automatic: the moment you push code to your `main` branch, it deploys to `qa.seatsync.com`. ***The Production pipeline, however, MUST be manual***. You should never accidentally trigger a deployment to live users just by saving a file. Production deployments should happen only when you click a button.

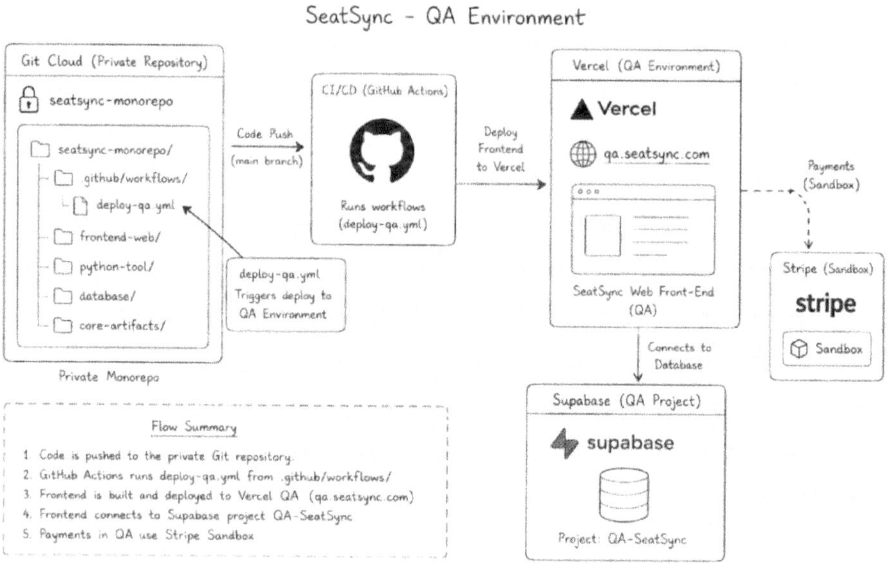

Fig 13-2

Example: Prompting for the QA Pipeline

Open a fresh AI chat window. Provide the Core Blueprint, and execute the following prompt:

INFRASTRUCTURE PROMPT - QA PIPELINE:

You are an expert DevOps Architect. We are building SeatSync using a monorepo structure.

Frontend: React/Next.js (/frontend-web)

Write a GitHub Actions CI/CD pipeline (deploy-qa.yml) with these rules:

1. Trigger automatically when code is pushed to the 'main' branch.

2. Only trigger if files in frontend-web or python-tools were changed.

3. Run our Jest unit tests. If tests fail, halt the deployment.

4. If tests pass, deploy the code to our Vercel QA environment using the Vercel CLI.

Provide secure, well-commented YAML code. Do not hardcode any secrets.

Action Steps: The Iterative Production Prompt

Step 1: Save the AI's response as `deploy-qa.yml` in your `.github/workflows/` folder. Test it by pushing a small code change and watching it deploy to QA automatically.
Step 2: Once QA works perfectly, do not ask the AI to guess the Production script from scratch. Give it the working script and use an iterative prompt:

INFRASTRUCTURE PROMPT - PROD PIPELINE:
Our QA pipeline works perfectly. Below is the YAML code.
[PASTE QA YAML]

Now, generate a new file called 'deploy-prod.yml'. It must use the exact same build and test steps, but with two critical changes:
1. It must NOT trigger automatically on a push. It must only trigger manually using 'workflow_dispatch'.
2. It must deploy to Vercel using the '--prod' flag.
Output the modified YAML.

By anchoring the AI to a known, working script, you guarantee consistency across your environments.

The Deployment Workflow: The Golden Path
You have structured the code, stood up the three cloud tiers, and written the automated pipelines. You now possess a professional, enterprise-grade deployment workflow. Let us walk through the exact lifecycle of releasing a new feature—for example, adding an 'Apple Pay' button to SeatSync.

Step 1: Local Dev & Sandbox Testing
Prompt your Front-End Virtual Team to write the Apple Pay component. You run the app on your laptop (`localhost:3000`), connected to your `SeatSync-Dev` Supabase database. You tweak the prompt until it works perfectly. Your local tests pass.

Step 2: Merge & Auto-Deploy to QA
You commit the code and push it to the `main` branch on GitHub. Your `deploy-qa.yml` Action automatically intercepts it, runs your test suite, and pushes the code to

`qa.seatsync.com` in Vercel. You log into the QA site, click the Apple Pay button, and verify it successfully talks to the Stripe Sandbox API. You sign off on the feature.

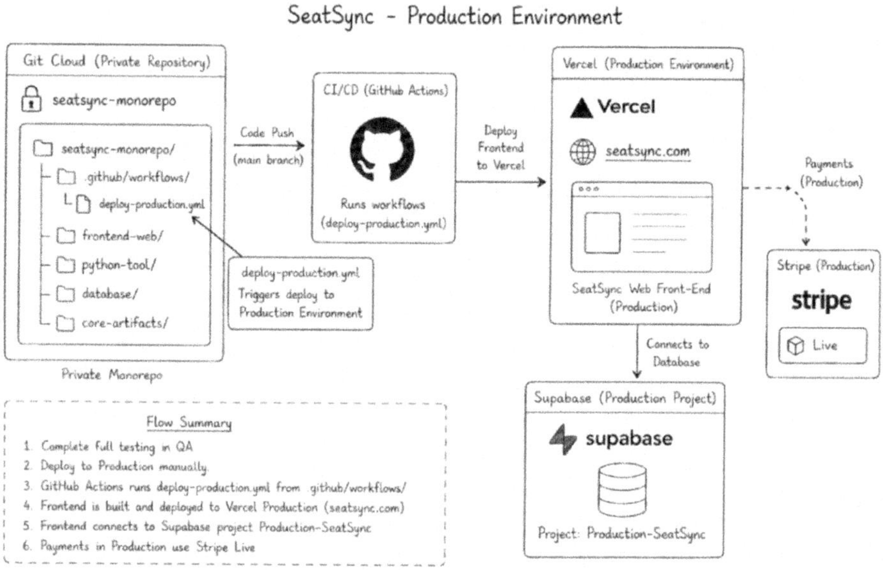

Fig 13-3

Step 3: Database Migration (Production)
Before pushing code to Production, you must ensure the live database is ready. If the Apple Pay feature required a new column in your database, you execute that SQL migration script against the `SeatSync-Prod` database now. You would need to use your Virtual Database team to generate this SQL migration code. You are making the SQL change manually in the Dev environment but you will use SQL script to make the same changes in the QA and Prod database.

Step 4: Manual Prod Trigger
You navigate to the 'Actions' tab in your GitHub repository. You select the `deploy-prod.yml` workflow and click the 'Run Workflow' button. The script takes the exact, verified code from your `main` branch and deploys it live. You visit `seatsync.com` to perform a final smoke test. The feature is live, and your users are happy.

Conclusion
Infrastructure and DevOps can sound intimidating, but by leveraging an isolated Virtual Team and adhering strictly to the principle of simplicity, you tame the complexity.
By moving your Development database to the cloud, protecting your blast radius with isolated environments, and establishing a split automatic/manual deployment pipeline, you have built a world-class delivery engine. You have eliminated deployment anxiety. You can now release code with the confidence of a massive engineering department, executed entirely by you and your AI virtual teams.
Your product is live. It is robust, secure, and actively serving users. But the journey of an entrepreneur does not end at launch. Software is a living, breathing entity. In the final chapter of this book, we will explore the Lean Machine—how to maintain your codebase, safely iterate on production features, and read server logs using AI. It is time to scale.

Chapter 14: The Lean Machine: Maintenance and Iteration

Launch day is not the finish line; it is merely the starting line. Many founders pop champagne on deployment day, only to be crushed by the weight of maintenance three months later. Software is not a static bridge you build and walk away from. It is a living, breathing organism that requires continuous feeding, pruning, and protection.
As a Solo Founder equipped with AI engineering departments, your leverage is unprecedented. However, the Software Development Life Cycle (SDLC) shifts dramatically once your application hits production. The operation, maintenance, enhancement, and support phases demand a different operational cadence. Your priority transitions from raw creation to disciplined curation. Making things easy to maintain and aggressively simple is the hallmark of longevity.
In this final chapter, we will explore the operational reality of the AI-augmented founder. We will discuss how to use AI as your on-call Site Reliability Engineer (SRE) to decode cryptic production logs, and how to safely push new features using the 5-team virtual structure you mastered earlier. Finally, we will step back and look at the philosophical and architectural horizon of generative AI, preparing you for the future of entrepreneurship.

The Post-Production Lifecycle for the Solo Founder
When SeatSync succeeds and thousands of users log in to book their coffee shop seats, your operational reality changes. You are no longer just an architect; you are the support team, the product manager, and the operations lead. This is the point you will have to hire developer(s) who will run, maintain, and enhance the software. You heard me right, this is the point, if you are successful, you will need to hire developer(s).

Maintaining an existing product is much more challenging than building a new product. I don't subscribe to the idea that all

programmers will lose their job due to AI. There will be need for developers but their role may evolve to multiple functions. However, the number of developers required in the market will be significantly less.
While an exhaustive guide to IT operations is beyond the scope of this book, here are the non-negotiable rules for managing this phase without burning out:

- *Automate Monitoring:* Never rely on users to tell you the site is down. Set up automated uptime alerts (e.g., BetterStack or Datadog) to alert you if your Vercel or Supabase instances fail.
- *Batch Your Bug Fixes:* Context switching is the enemy of the solo founder. Do not immediately fix every minor visual glitch. Log them in a tracking board and deploy bug fixes in batches once a week.
- *Ruthless Feature Prioritization:* Users will request a hundred new features. Only build those that directly reduce churn or increase revenue. Your AI can build anything, but your architecture cannot sustain everything.
- *Protect the Data Pipeline:* Backups are your ultimate insurance policy. Ensure your Supabase production environment is running automated daily backups, and test restoring them quarterly.

AI as Your On-Call Engineer: Reading Production Logs

In traditional software engineering, debugging a production error involves hours of sifting through massive text files filled with cryptic timestamps, server metrics, and stack traces. It is tedious, demoralizing work. As an AI-augmented founder, you will outsource this entirely - to AI.

Concept: Log Parsing via AI

Large Language Models are fundamentally pattern-matching engines. This makes them extraordinarily gifted at spotting anomalies in structured data, such as server logs. When SeatSync throws a '500 Internal Server Error', your first step is no longer Googling the error code. Your first step is feeding the log to your AI.

Example: The SeatSync Latency Spike
Imagine it is a busy Tuesday morning. Users are complaining that SeatSync is taking ten seconds to load available seats. You check your Vercel logs and see a massive wall of text detailing database query times and memory limits. To the untrained eye, it is noise.
You copy the last 50 lines of the log. Before doing anything else, you scrub any Personally Identifiable Information (PII)—like user email addresses or session tokens—replacing them with asterisks. Then, you open a fresh chat window.

Action Steps: The Diagnostics Prompt
Use the following framework to turn your AI into a senior SRE:
• Step 1: Export the logs from your hosting provider (Vercel/Supabase).
• Step 2: Sanitize the logs. Never paste live user data or production secrets into an AI prompt.
• Step 3: Use an expert persona prompt to extract the root cause.
DIAGNOSTICS PROMPT:
You are an expert Site Reliability Engineer (SRE) and Database Administrator.
Below is an anonymized production log dump from our Vercel Next.js edge functions and Supabase database. Our users are experiencing 10-second latency spikes when loading the seat availability component.

[PASTE SANITIZED LOGS]

Task:
1. Identify the specific process or query causing the bottleneck.
2. Explain why it is failing in plain English.
3. Provide three actionable solutions to fix this, ranked from easiest to implement to most robust.
The AI will instantly read through the noise. It might reply: "The logs indicate a missing database index on the 'reservations' table. Every time a user loads the page,

Supabase is performing a full sequential scan of all 50,000 reservations. Solution 1: Run this SQL command to create an index on 'shop_id'." You test the fix in your QA environment, deploy it, and the latency drops to 50 milliseconds.

Safely Pushing Updates: Re-engaging the Virtual Teams
Your product is stable, but a new competitor emerges. You need to iterate. You want to add a 'User Reviews' feature so people can rate the Wi-Fi at each coffee shop. How do you integrate this massive new feature into a live, production codebase without breaking the existing reservation system?

Concept: The 5-Team Iteration Loop
You rely on the exact same 5-team chat structure we built in Chapter 3 (Architecture, Database & Back-end, Front-end, DevOps, and Product Marketing). You do not start hacking away in your existing codebase. You spin up the virtual teams, update the blueprints, and follow the pipeline.

Example: Adding User Reviews to SeatSync
You do not open your laptop and start coding. You open your 'Architect Virtual Team' chat. You paste your current Core Blueprint and your Interface Contract. You tell the Architect you want to add a Review system. The Architect updates the Blueprint, creating a new 'Reviews' table and a new Edge Function.

Action Steps: The Feature Deployment Pipeline
Step 1: Update the Core Artifacts. Use the Architect team to update the Blueprint with the new database schema. Execute this schema in your local Development database.
Step 2: Backend Isolation. Spin up the Database & Back-end Team. Give it the updated Blueprint. Make it generate the new Edge FunctionTest locally.
Step 3: Frontend Integration. Spin up the Frontend Virtual Team. Have it build the UI components. Test locally against the new backend.
Step 4: The Staging Pipeline. Push the code to GitHub. Your CI/CD pipeline deploys it to your QA environment

(`qa.seatsync.com`). You run the database migration on the QA Supabase instance. You test it thoroughly.
Step 5: Production Launch. Run the database migration on the Production Supabase instance. Manually trigger the production deployment. The feature is live, and your core reservation system remains perfectly intact.

Final Thoughts: The Future of the AI-Augmented Entrepreneur

As we close this book, I must ask you to shift your perspective. Remove the hat of the practical engineer, and put on the hat of the AI scientist and philosopher. We must look at what this technology actually is, its fundamental limitations, and what the next decade holds for you as an entrepreneur.

The Illusion of Thought vs. Stochastic Prediction

When you spend hours conversing with an LLM, it feels distinctly like you are talking to a colleague. It is polite, it is creative, and it writes brilliant code. I must remind you of the architectural reality: *Generative AI does not 'think'. It does not 'know' anything in the human sense.*
At its core, an *LLM is a massively complex statistical engine performing Next-Token Prediction.* It is an autoregressive model. Given the context of your prompt, it calculates the highest mathematical probability for the next word, and then the next. It is a *'stochastic parrot.'*

The Architectural Limitation: Hallucination is a Feature

Understanding this architecture is crucial because it reveals a hard limitation: Hallucinations are not bugs that can be entirely patched out; they are the fundamental feature of the model's creativity. The exact same mechanism that allows the AI to invent a clever, novel solution to a coding problem is the mechanism that causes it to invent a phantom library that does not exist. You cannot have the boundless creativity without the probabilistic risk.
Furthermore, despite rapidly expanding Context Windows (from 4,000 tokens a few years ago to millions today), the 'Lost in the Middle' problem persists. The models struggle with

deep, multi-step logical reasoning over vast distances of text because their attention mechanisms spread too thin.

The Enduring Value of the Human Architect

What does this mean for the future of AI development and the solo founder? Over the next five to ten years, AI will not replace the entrepreneur. It will not spontaneously build, launch, and maintain profitable businesses entirely on its own. All successful products will need developers to keep the ship floating. The developer role will probably evolve into a multi role which will include code review, QA, Site Reliability Engineer (SRE) and a SME (Subject Matter Expert). This new role is immensely good fit for them. In this new role they will probably have more job security. A company turning over 10-20 millions of dollars will probably only need 2-3 of these new roles.

The models will become faster, multimodal, and integrated into agents that can execute terminal commands, interact with websites. But they will still lack intent, systemic taste, and life experience, ability to distinguish truth from falsehood. Generative AI will ignite a new era of innovation and a curious, disciplined individual with minimal exposure to software development can harness this capability to turn a value proposition to a running business. This book is an attempt to deliver this new capability to everyone who want to give it a try. The barrier to a software product development has been significantly reduced. So has the cost of failure. You can be a AI-augmented entrepreneur, the 'solo founder'. The tide is right. Go build.

Contact the author

If you are a reader with no prior coding experience, you may contact the author with questions or training inquiries at:

https://llm-psyche.lovable.app/

APPENDIX A: LIST OF DOCUMENTS USED IN THIS BOOK

APPENDIX B: BUILDING YOUR OWN TOOL TO TRACK TOKEN USAGE

1. Pre-requisites:

1. You must have installed Python on your windows system. Your PATH variable points to Python installation directory.
2. You have a folder called c:\temp\token-analyzer on your system
3. You have carefully copy pasted your entire chat conversation, including your prompts and AI platforms response in a file called 'virtual-team-chat.txt' located at c:\temp\token-analyzer

2. Building your own Python tool called 'token-tracker.py'
Example prompt to generate the tool, use with any AI platform:

The Persona:
You are an elite AI token management engineer. Your design principle is
always simplicity first. You are very skilled in python coding. I am experienced application Architect.

The Context:
I want you to write a python tool called 'token_analyzer.py' to analyze the token usage in an AI chat conversation. This code will run on windows but should be easily runnable on apple OS with minimum or no change.
The Intent:
I have already copied my entire conversation in a AI chat to a text file located on my windows pc at:
C:/temp/token-analyzer/input-team-chat.txt

Have a configuration section in token_analyzer.py and store following reusable configuration there. You will be using this configuration information for analyzing the chat history:
input_output_path = c:\temp\token-analyzer

input_file = input-team-chat.txt
output_file = token_analysis_report_date_time.txt
Low risk : 0–8K tokens
Medium risk: 8K–32K tokens
High risk: 32K+ tokens
1 word = 1.2 -1.4 tokens
1 page = 260-330 tokens

The Output Format:
You will use the total number of tokens calculated and classify the risk of hallucination according to the threshold in the configuration section. Report and calculate everything using tokens only.

APPENDIX B: Continued

To make the output easier to understand by humans you will report the total token count and the number pages that means. Your output will include a warning 'The hallucination thresholds are different for different LLM Models. Please adjust the configuration values by trial and error for your LLM.'
You will generate the analysis report in text file c:\temp\token-analyzer\token_analysis_report_date_time.txt
The date and time will be part of the output file name to ensure the report names are unique and those files are not overwritten.
Ask me clarifying question before generating the code.

3. Running your tool token-tracker.py

Copy the generated code in a to a file called token-tracker.py then run the script as follows:

Place token_analyzer.py and input-team-chat.txt in the exact same folder c:\temp\token-analyzer.
Open your terminal or command prompt.

Navigate to that folder in command prompt (e.g., c:\temp\token-analyzer).
Run the script: *python token_analyzer.py*
The script will instantly output a unique file like token_analysis_report_20260624_121616.txt in same folder.

APPENDIX C: SETTING UP YOUR SUPABASE ENVIRONMENT

Use following prompt to get step by step instructions from any major AI platform like Gemini or ChatGPT. To save tokens do not put this prompt in any of your virtual team chat but open a new chat window for this. Save the generated instructions for future use.
Example Prompt:

The Persona: You are a top infrastructure engineer working at Supabase. You have access to all their latest documentation. You verify all set up instructions you generate against the latest Supabase documentation.
The Context: I am an application developer trying to set up and Development environment in Supabase. I plan to use Postgres for my web application as database and RLS security by default from my Web frontend on my PC.
The Intent: Please provide me detailed step by step instructions for setting up my development environment in Supabase. Please also provide instructions for connecting my Development Web frontend from my PC to Supabase.
The Output Format: Output the instructions in a checklist format. Ask clarifying questions before generating the instructions.

To economize tokens you can remove the words '*The Persona:*', '*The Context:*', '*The Intent:*', '*The Output Format:* ' from your actual prompt.

You can use a very similar prompt to set up your Vercel QA and Production environments.

APPENDIX D: INSTALLING GIT USING PROMPT ENGINEERING:

The Persona: You are security conscious a top DevOps engineer. You love to keep things simple.

The Context: I am a new developer trying to install Git on my local [Windows PC /Apple PC]. I will use this local Git as my development environment. I will be using Visual Studio Code for writing the code. I have already installed Visual Studio Code locally.

The Intent: I want to install a local Git and connect a new private project called [MYAPP1] in GitHub. I want to set up a simple Mono Repo . My local folder structure will look like this:

MYAPP1-monorepo/
├── .github/workflows/   (Automated CI/CD deployment scripts)
├── frontend-web/   (React/Next.js code - deployed to Vercel)
├── python-tools/   (Python Tool / future python components)
├── database/   (Supabase SQL migration files)
└── core-artifacts/   (Documentations: Core Blueprint, Interface Contracts)

The Output Format: Please provide me step by step instructions in a checklist format to install the local Git , connect it my GitHub project and Visual Studio code and a simple test to confirm everything is working.

APPENDIX E: GENRATE YOUR PYTHON CODE REVIEW TOOL

Whenever you ask AI to generate a full code file you run the risk of the AI refactoring the code even removing a working section from your code. So when you need to update code file ask the AI to only the change the part of the code 'surgically' and give you only that change for plugging in the code in your Visual Studio Code files. In case you have had to ask Ai to generate a full code file then you must do 'code review'. To do that use the python tool generated by following prompt to compare the older code file and the new code file for changes made. Review these changes carefully before accepting the new code. This where many AI coding project go bad. Prompt example:

The Persona: You are skilled Python developer. You are specially good at comparing code files for changes as apart of code review. You love to keep things simple.

The Context:
I need to compare existing code file called reservation.ts (source) to a file called new_ reservation.ts (target)
Both files are located in following folder:
C:\temp\my_code_review
I want the this code to be reusable have configuration section in the code where I can change the paths and names of the source and target file.

The Intent: I want to know the lines that were deleted, changed and added in target file compared to the source file.

The Output Format:

Generate a Python code file called 'code_reviewer.py' that will compare the source and target files and output report called 'code_reviewe_report.txt' in the same folder as the target file. This report file will contain:
Date and time when it was run.
Who ran the report.
Source file name with location.
Target file name with location.
List of lines missing in target file with their line number in source file.
List of lines changed in target file with their line number in target file.
List of lines added in target file with their line number in target file.
Total number of changes.

APPENDIX F: REFERENCES & BIBLIOGRAPHY

This appendix compiles the seminal academic research, foundational business frameworks, and corporate culture documentation referenced throughout The Art of Prompt Engineering for Solo Founders. These works anchor the validation workflows in Part I and the token context economy optimization methods developed in Part III.

Foundational Strategy & Ideation Frameworks

Barney, J. (1991). Firm resources and sustained competitive advantage. Journal of Management, 17(1), 99–120. https://doi.org/10.1177/014920639101700108

Blank, S. (2003). The Four Steps to the Epiphany: Successful Strategies for Products that Win. K&S Ranch Publishing.

Christensen, C. M. (2016). Competing Against Luck: The Story of Innovation and Customer Choice. Harper Business.

Ries, E. (2011). The Lean Startup: How Today's Entrepreneurs Use Continuous Innovation to Create Radically Successful Businesses. Crown Business.

Corporate Strategy Letters & Culture Frameworks

Bezos, J. (2016). 2016 Letter to Shareholders. Amazon.com, Inc.

Netflix, Inc. (2024). Netflix Culture Memo: Seeking Excellence. Netflix Jobs.
https://jobs.netflix.com/culture

Large Language Model & Context Window Engineering Research

Liu, N. F., Lin, K., Hewitt, J., Paranjape, A., Bevilacqua, M., Petroni, F., & Liang, P.
(2024). Lost in the Middle: How Language Models Use Long Contexts. Transactions of the Association for Computational Linguistics, 12, 157–173.
https://doi.org/10.1162/tacl_a_00638
Cited by: 4797

Liu, S., Halder, K., Qi, Z., Xiao, W., Pappas, N., Htut, P. M., John, N. A., Benajiba, Y., & Roth,
D. (2025). Towards Long Context Hallucination Detection. arXiv.
https://doi.org/10.48550/arxiv.2504.19457
Cited by: 22

www.ingramcontent.com/pod-product-compliance
Ingram Content Group UK Ltd.
Pitfield, Milton Keynes, MK11 3LW, UK
UKHW021405110926
15112UKWH00018B/150

9 798234 131942